TAXES AND GROWTH
BUSINESS INCENTIVES AND
ECONOMIC DEVELOPMENT

STUDIES IN DEVELOPMENT POLICY
Michael Barker, General Editor

1. *State Taxation and Economic Development* by Roger J. Vaughan
2. *Economic Development: Challenge of the 1980s* by Neal Peirce, Jerry Hagstrom, and Carol Steinbach
3. *Innovations in Development Finance* by Lawrence Litvak and Belden Daniels
4. *The Working Poor: Towards a State Agenda* by David M. Gordon
5. *Inflation and Unemployment* by Roger J. Vaughan
6. *Democratizing the Development Process* by Neal Peirce, Jerry Hagstrom, and Carol Steinbach
7. *Venture Capital and Urban Development* by Michael Kieschnick
8. *Development Politics: Private Development and the Public Interest* by Robert Hollister and Tunney Lee
9. *The Capital Budget* by Robert DeVoy and Harold Wise
10. *Banking and Small Business* by Derek Hansen
11. *Taxes and Growth: Business Incentives and Economic Development* by Michael Kieschnick
12. *Pension Funds and Economic Renewal* by Lawrence Litvak
13. *The Road to 1984: Beyond Supply Side Economics* by Roger J. Vaughan

Also published by the Council:

POLICY PAPERS
Michael Barker, General Editor

1. *Economic Renewal: A Guide for the Perplexed*
2. *The Employment and Training System: What's wrong with it and how to fix it*
3. *State Regulation and Economic Development*
4. *Industrial Policy*
5. *Financing Entrepreneurship*
6. *State and Local Investment Strategies*
7. *Monetary Policy*
8. *Social Security: Why it's in trouble and what can be done about it*
9. *Pension Funds and the Housing Problem*

STUDIES IN RENEWABLE RESOURCE POLICY
Michael Barker, General Editor

1. *State Conservation and Solar Energy Tax Programs* by Leonard Rodberg and Meg Schachter
2. *Environmental Quality and Economic Growth* by Robert Hamrin

America in Ruins: Beyond the Public Works Pork Barrel by Pat Choate and Susan Walter

TAXES AND GROWTH
BUSINESS INCENTIVES AND ECONOMIC DEVELOPMENT

MICHAEL KIESCHNICK

VOLUME ELEVEN
STUDIES IN DEVELOPMENT POLICY
MICHAEL BARKER, GENERAL EDITOR

336.2
K 47t

Am

COVER: "Map 1963," by Jasper Johns. Collection Albert Saalsfield. Grateful
acknowledgement is made to Mr. Johns for allowing the reproduction of
this work.

Partial funding support for this volume was received from the Division of Economic
Research, Economic Development Administration, the U.S. Department of
Commerce. The views and findings it contains are the author's, and do not necessarily
represent those of the Economic Development Administration or the members or staff
of the Council of State Planning Agencies. Reproduction of any part of this volume is
permitted for any purpose of the United States Government.

Library of Congress Catalog Number: 81-82979

ISBN: 0-934842-09-4

Printed in the United States of America. First edition - 1981

CONTENTS

TABLES

TABLES IN APPENDICES

PREFACE AND ACKNOWLEDGMENTS

There is an overwhelming desire at the state and local level to do something about economic stagnation and underdevelopment. Elected officials and development planners rarely have a mandate to simply sit by and watch private (not necessarily market) forces dictate the pace and composition of economic development. Businesses and their trade organizations continually ask for lower taxes or special incentives, always promising that the tax cut will prove self-financing through its stimulus to private taxable activities. Usually at least one of the neighboring (competing?) states has lower taxes or greater incentives, and will be pointed to as the possible location for all future expansions. At least one legislator is always willing to introduce a measure calling for tax incentives to retain firms or boost the economy. Most elected officials, whether in the executive branch or the legislature, face such situations frequently. They rarely know what to do, nor do they have the time or resources to attempt any analytical study of the pros and cons of relying on state tax incentives as an integral part of their development policy. This book is intended to make life a bit easier for them and a bit harder for those who promise too much from tax incentives.

Perhaps no book has been begun with such confidence and left with such humility. Much of the research that serves as the core of this book was done during late evenings and scattered weekends. This time was available only due to the patience of my wife, Meg Schachter, who also offered both methodological and editorial comments of great value. Roger Vaughan provided substantial review throughout the process, and several sections owe a great deal to him. Susan Green was very helpful in getting out the mail survey, while Julie DeMayo did a large amount of "number crunching" on the 1980 interstate tax comparisons. Herman "Dutch" Leonard offered help in methodological aspects of the econometric work. Elaine Sorensen provided critical assistance in all aspects of the mail survey and econometric investigations, and the book would still not be done without her. Michael Barker, of the Council of State Planning Agencies, was foolish enough to let me suggest and then pursue this topic, but was extremely patient and helpful in obtaining background information and in editing the final version. All of the remaining errors—for there must be some I missed—remain my responsibility.

INTRODUCTION

Since the early years of U.S. economic history, state governments have sought to influence the pace and composition of economic development. Over time, they have used tax policy, regulatory policies, direct expenditures and public persuasion in efforts to increase income and employment for state residents. These policies have received mixed support from both economists and the businesses they are intended to benefit.

After a decade of slow economic growth, an increasing number of states are turning to manipulations of their overall tax structure and explicit tax incentives to induce industrial development. Hardly a legislative session goes by in each state without a new tax incentive proposal being debated and quite frequently adopted.

A tax incentive represents the expenditure of public funds for economic development purposes. As such, its costs and benefits need to be evaluated just as one would evaluate public works, job training programs, or direct loans to businesses. Proponents of tax incentives have argued that taxes are an important barrier to business expansion, and that tax reductions can be targeted to investment or employment increases to stimulate development. Opponents have argued that taxes at the state and local level are of little importance in business investment decisions, so that tax incentives represent windfalls to businesses which would have invested or hired in any case.

With a few notable exceptions, academic economists have opposed the use of state tax incentives, characterizing them as ineffective. Even if incentives are effective in influencing the location of investments, many economists condemn them as leading to a misallocation of resources. For the most part, the vigor of economists' verbal opposition has been overwhelmed by the interests of state legislators and their business constituents in adding to the number of incentives. A few economists, focusing on the competition among states for new businesses, have concluded that the provision of subsidies under competition leads to an improved allocation of resources— particularly labor—and should be encouraged and expanded in depth.

For the most part, this study will assume that the broad goals of development policy are agreed upon—an increase of employment and income for in-state residents. Largely ignored will be issues of the quality and distribution of employment opportunities among individuals or communities within the state. To render the study manageable, the examination of policies will be limited to attempts by states to use specific automatic provisions within their state corporate income tax to influence business investment decisions. The policy question addressed in this study is, "Should a state, given its present tax levels and structure, its present expenditure policy, and its present regulatory policy, adopt tax incentives intended to increase business investment within its borders?"

The study combines a conceptual essay, a review of the academic literature, and new empirical work. While the existing literature is voluminous, most is conceptually or methodologically flawed, and is better presented within the context of a more appropriate framework. The study consists of five chapters. Chapter One presents an overview of the level and composition of present state and local taxes, along with a review of existing state business tax incentives. Chapter Two considers the use of tax incentives as a public investment in a benefit/cost framework. Chapter Three is a literature review of existing empirical studies on the effects of state business tax incentives. Chapter Four presents new empirical research developed as part of this study. Finally, Chapter Five summarizes the findings and considers the implications of the study for state policymakers.

1

THE STRUCTURE OF STATE TAX SYSTEMS

Researchers seeking analytical simplicity would do well to avoid the field of state taxation of business. The number of different taxes, tax base definitions, and lack of publicly available data present far more difficulties than are found in federal taxation.

As can be seen in Table 1 below, the relative importance of particular taxes has changed quite dramatically at the state level over the past decades. In particular, the state property tax has declined to the extent that property tax revenues are now overwhelmingly a local revenue source. States have significantly increased the use of general and selective sales taxes. Personal income taxes have steadily increased in importance. As a percentage of state revenues, the corporate income tax has remained relatively stable, generally fluctuating between 5 and 9 percent.

THE ISSUE OF TAX INCIDENCE It is well understood by most economists, but very few political figures, that the entity which writes the check to the state Department of Finance is not necessarily the same entity which bears the tax burden. There is extraordinary disagreement over the incidence of corporate income taxes, with some arguing that all corporate income taxes are a burden on shareholders, others arguing that such taxes are shifted forward to consumers, and others arguing a more eclectic position—with the burden shared among shareholders, consumers, and workers depending on characteristics of the relevant factor and demand markets. If all state/local taxes on businesses are shifted forward to consumers, state tax incentives should have little or no incentive effect. If they are all borne by shareholders, there may be a significant incentive effect from reducing such taxes.

The issue of incidence substantially complicates the task of apportioning the state and local tax burden between individuals and businesses for purposes of interstate tax comparisons. The Advisory Commission on Intergovernmental Relations (hereafter ACIR) has periodically issued estimates of the amounts of state and local taxes initially paid by businesses, carefully avoiding the issue of eventual incidence. Their estimates considering the states as a whole are displayed in Table 2 below. The share of taxes initially paid by business has declined from 36.8 percent in 1957 to 30.6 percent in 1977. Over the

Table 1

State Taxes by Source—Selected Years 1940–1980
(In Percent)

Year	Total Excluding Unemployment Taxes	Individual Income Taxes	Corporate Income Taxes	Death and Gift Taxes	General Sales Taxes	Selective Sales Taxes	Property Taxes	Motor Vehicle Licences	All Other
1940	100.0%	6.2%	4.7%	3.4%	15.1%	34.0%	7.8%	11.7%	17.0%
1950	100.0	9.1	7.4	2.1	21.0	33.8	3.9	9.5	13.1
1960	100.0	12.2	6.5	2.3	23.9	28.8	3.4	8.7	12.1
1962	100.0	13.3	6.4	2.5	24.9	30.4	3.1	8.1	11.6
1964	100.0	14.1	7.0	2.7	25.1	28.9	3.0	7.9	11.4
1966	100.0	14.6	6.9	2.8	26.8	27.7	2.8	7.6	10.8
1968	100.0	17.1	6.9	2.4	28.7	25.6	2.5	6.8	9.9
1970	100.0	19.1	7.8	2.1	29.6	24.0	2.3	6.2	9.0
1972	100.0	21.7	7.4	2.2	29.4	22.7	2.1	5.6	8.9
1974	100.0	23.0	8.1	1.9	30.5	21.1	1.8	5.1	8.7
1976	100.0	24.0	8.1	1.7	30.6	19.2	2.4	4.9	9.0
1978	100.0	25.7	9.5	1.6	31.1	16.6	2.1	4.3	9.0
1980 (Est.)	100.0	26.4	9.7	1.5	31.6	15.3	1.9	4.0	9.6

SOURCE: Table 52, *Significant Features of Fiscal Federalism: 1979–1980 Edition*, M-123, Advisory Commission on Intergovernmental Relations, Washington, D.C., October, 1980.

Table 2

State and Local Taxes with an Initial Impact on Business
By Type of Tax 1957, 1962, 1967, 1977

Tax	Amount (in millions)				Percent of Total			
	1977	1967	1962	1957	1977	1967	1962	1957
Total, excluding unemployment taxes	$53,520	$19,900	$14,478	$10,553	100.0%	100.0%	100.0%	100.0%
Property (real and personal)	21,288	10,298	8,156	5,808	39.8	51.7	56.3	55.0
Sales and Gross Receipts	15,062	4,076	2,694	1,902	28.1	20.5	18.6	18.0
Corporate Net Income	9,902	2,479	1,332	1,043	18.5	12.5	9.2	9.9
Severance	2,168	577	451	388	4.1	2.9	3.1	3.7
License and other	5,100	2,470	1,845	1,412	9.5	12.4	12.7	13.4

SOURCE: Table A-1, *Regional Growth: Interstate Tax Competition*, Report A-76, Advisory Commission on Intergovernmental Relations, Washington, D.C., March 1981.

7

past twenty years, property taxes on businesses have declined in relative importance but remain the single largest tax. Sales taxes paid by business and corporate income taxes have generally increased. For the most part, the income and sales taxes are state levies while the property taxes are local levies. Unemployment taxes are relatively large, but are levied on crudely determined actuarial grounds, and so are relatively less important determinants of interstate tax differentials.

When disaggregated, as in Table 3 below, it is clear that the share of state and local taxes paid by business varies significantly among states. In West Virginia, businesses pay 45.4 percent of state/local taxes, while in Nebraska, businesses pay only 19.0 percent of state/local taxes.

RELATIVE IMPORTANCE OF STATE/LOCAL TAXES ON BUSINESS

As a share of sales or income, or relative to some base such as employment, how important are state and local taxes initally borne by business?

As shown in Table 4 below, there are substantial differences among states in terms of the tax burden per employee. In 1977, Alaska imposed about $4,273 per private nonagricultural employee, while South Carolina imposed only about $475. Alaska is clearly an extraordinary case, with only six other states imposing a burden of over $1,000 per employee. The median tax burden per employee in 1977 was $669. Such figures do not accurately represent the tax burden of any single employer, since firms in different industries have very different capital/labor ratios, profitability, and other factors which influence relative tax burden.

For manufacturing firms, it is possible to construct a "hypothetical" firm, complete with balance sheets and income statements, with which to calculate the state and local taxes which would be paid in each state. The results of one such study are shown in Table 5 below. In 1980, the hypothetical firm would have had an average (unweighted) state and local tax burden of $184,798 on sales of $6,919,920 (or 2.7 percent of sales). This reflects quite a wide range, with North Dakota imposing $892,070 (with the great majority in local property taxes) and Nevada only $59,340.

Much of this variation reflects the differences in local property tax rates. However, there is also substantial variation among states in the corporate income tax structure. As seen in Table 6, a number of states do not tax corporate income at all (Wyoming, Washington, Texas, South Dakota, Nevada). Among states with proportionate taxation, the rate varies from 3 to 12 percent. Among states with progressive corporate tax structures, the rate varies from 1 to 10.5 percent. The base for determining taxable income also varies substantially. Alabama,

Table 3

Taxes With an Initial Impact on Business as A Share of Total State and Local Taxes[1]

Ranked in Decreasing Order of Percent Share

1977

1.	West Virginia	45.4%	27.	Pennsylvania	29.4
2.	Alaska	42.5	28.	North Carolina	29.1
3.	Wyoming	39.2	29.	Virginia	28.4
4.	Tennessee	34.9	30.	Idaho	27.6
5.	Washington	34.5	31.	Utah	27.5
6.	Delaware	34.2	32.	Oregon	27.5
7.	Connecticut	33.4	33.	Rhode Island	26.9
8.	Texas	33.0	34.	Vermont	26.6
9.	Kansas	32.9	35.	Arkansas	26.5
10.	Ohio	32.8	36.	South Carolina	26.1
11.	Alabama	32.0	37.	Georgia	25.7
12.	Illinois	32.0	38.	Hawaii	25.3
13.	D.C.	31.9	39.	New Mexico	25.0
14.	Arizona	31.8	40.	Maine	24.6
15.	Missouri	31.2	41.	Minnesota	24.5
16.	Florida	30.9	42.	Maryland	24.1
17.	California	30.9	43.	Oklahoma	23.7
18.	Colorado	30.7	44.	Massachusetts	23.6
19.	Nevada	30.4	45.	Michigan	23.5
20.	New York	30.4	46.	North Dakota	23.4
21.	New Hampshire	30.1	47.	Kentucky	23.3
22.	Montana	29.9	48.	South Dakota	22.1
23.	Louisiana	29.8	49.	Iowa	21.5
24.	New Jersey	29.8	50.	Wisconsin	22.3
25.	Mississippi	29.7	51.	Nebraska	19.0
26.	Indiana	29.6			

[1]Excluding severance taxes

SOURCE: Business taxes, excluding severance taxes, derived from Table A-2, *Regional Growth: Interstate Tax Competition.*

Arizona, Iowa, Louisiana, Missouri, and North Dakota allow a firm to deduct all or part of its federal tax liability in arriving at state taxable income. Most states simply adopt the federal definition of taxable income, thus incorporating federal depreciation provisions, while some begin with sales and use separate (and frequently unique) depreciation provisions.

States also differ in the manner in which they determine taxable income for those corporations whose activities are spread among a

Table 4

Business Taxes per Nonagricultural Private Employee Ranked in Decreasing Order

1977

1.	Alaska	$4,273	27.	Virginia	$ 667
2.	New York	1,221	28.	Nevada	664
3.	Wyoming	1,185	29.	North Dakota	636
4.	California	1,074	30.	Idaho	629
5.	Arizona	1,058	31.	Ohio	627
6.	West Virginia	1,049	32.	Tennessee	623
7.	Washington	937	33.	Mississippi	621
8.	Montana	893	34.	Rhode Island	615
9.	New Jersey	867	35.	New Mexico	611
10.	Delaware	836	36.	Utah	609
11.	Hawaii	807	37.	Wisconsin	597
12.	Kansas	802	38.	Alabama	594
13.	Colorado	791	39.	Missouri	591
14.	Illinois	787	40.	Indiana	582
15.	D.C.	779	41.	Maine	567
16.	Maryland	765	42.	New Hampshire	558
17.	Connecticut	762	43.	South Dakota	536
18.	Vermont	722	44.	North Carolina	529
19.	Florida	697	45.	Iowa	528
20.	Oregon	692	46.	Oklahoma	526
21.	Pennsylvania	692	47.	Kentucky	517
22.	Massachusetts	687	48.	Georgia	513
23.	Minnesota	674	49.	Arkansas	497
24.	Michigan	672	50.	Nebraska	495
25.	Louisiana	670	51.	South Carolina	475
26.	Texas	669			

SOURCE: Business taxes, excluding severance taxes, derived from Table A-2, *Regional Growth: Interstate Tax Competition.* Private employment taken from Table 1, "Employees on nonagricultural payrolls for states and selected areas by industry division," various issues, *Employment and Earnings,* U.S. Department of Labor, Bureau of Labor Statistics.

Table 5

Ranking of States by State and Local
Tax Burden on a Hypothetical
Average Manufacturing Corporation

1980

State	Tax Liability	State	Tax Liability
1. North Dakota	$892,070	27. Montana	$150,660
2. South Carolina	443,960	28. Maine	147,980
3. Massachusetts	387,630	29. Hawaii	144,950
4. New York	378,840	30. West Virginia	143,100
5. Rhode Island	325,900	31. Nebraska	141,700
6. Pennsylvania	325,720	32. Oregon	141,120
7. Mississippi	273,640	33. Idaho	138,300
8. Connecticut	270,120	34. Delaware	136,070
9. Kansas	229,110	35. Illinois	130,530
10. Indiana	226,800	36. Colorado	125,500
11. New Hampshire	214,640	37. South Dakota	123,840
12. Wisconsin	209,580	38. Florida	121,170
13. Vermont	209,000	39. Alaska	116,230
14. Iowa	199,620	40. Michigan	107,800
15. Virginia	196,390	41. Arkansas	107,700
16. New Jersey	188,920	42. North Carolina	103,360
17. Ohio	188,420	43. Utah	94,720
18. D.C.	180,800	44. Washington	93,530
19. California	171,510	45. New Mexico	89,830
20. Texas	170,920	46. Oklahoma	89,650
21. Missouri	161,780	47. Kentucky	80,000
22. Georgia	160,790	48. Louisiana	77,480
23. Tennessee	160,430	49. Alabama	65,770
24. Maryland	157,100	50. Wyoming	63,640
25. Minnesota	155,910	51. Nevada	59,340
26. Arizona	151,130		

SOURCE: Calculated on the basis of a hypothetical manufacturing firm with gross sales of $6,919,920. Details are available in Appendix I. Tax rates and methods based on *All States Tax Handbook,* 1980. The calculations do *not* include the effects of temporary tax incentives.

number of states (and sometimes countries). Most states allocate income for a multistate company according to a formula based on sales, employment, and assets. Typically, national (or worldwide) income is allocated to a state based on a formula using the share of the firm's total employment, sales, and assets which are located within the state. The weight attached to each factor varies, although the most common weighting procedure uses even weights. If all states allocated income in the same manner, all companies would pay taxes on 100 percent of their income, although at different rates in different states. As will be discussed in greater detail in Chapter 3, the existence of multistate firms, and the ambiguity over defining their actual income in a given state, tremendously complicates the development of an accurate measure of state tax burdens (and hence a measure of interstate differences). Equally profitable firms as measured nationally can be treated quite differently in the same state because of a different interstate allocation of out-of-state assets, sales, or employees.

THE BENEFIT SIDE OF TAXES   Most studies which attempt to relate state taxation to investment or location behavior neglect the benefits which businesses receive from state and local expenditures. The use of tax funds to train workers in schools and provide for highways and public protection all benefit businesses. Hence, differences in tax rates in some way reflect differences in service levels. However, taxes are also used for redistributive purposes and for activities which do not benefit businesses. If the relationship between tax burden and services was on an accurate fee-for-service basis, a firm could choose its location at least partially based on the cost per unit of services and on the state capacity to provide those services.

States differ dramatically in their mix of expenditures (see Table 7 below), while businesses certainly differ in their need for services. Some firms depend heavily on workers trained in public schools, while others are dependent on public highways. Others may prefer workers with little education at lower wages, or ship by rail. Few businesses demand higher welfare expenditures, although the welfare system may serve to support low-income workers who are frequently laid off from cyclical industries. As a percentage of state personal income, there are dramatic differences in state redistributive expenditures on welfare (see Table 7). An ideal analysis of taxation and industrial development must either adjust the tax level for redistributive expenditures, or include them in a separate analysis.

POSSIBLE INCENTIVE EFFECTS OF STATE TAXATION OF BUSINESS   As a byproduct of its revenue-generating function, state and local taxation may affect the economic decisions of businesses and households. While it is relatively easy to conceptually identify these incentive effects, it is far more difficult to quantify them. In the absence of empirical estimates of the responsiveness of various economic decisions to specific taxes, this

Table 6

State Corporate Income Tax Rates: 1980

State	Rate (%)	State	Rate (%)
Alabama	5.0	Montana	6.75
Alaska	5.4 (+4.0)*	Nebraska	4.5–4.95
Arizona	2.5–10.5	Nevada	—
Arkansas	1–6	New Hampshire	8.0
California	9.6	New Jersey	7.5
Colorado	5.0	New Mexico	5.0
Connecticut	10.0	New York	10.0
Delaware	8.7	North Carolina	6.0
D.C.	9.0**	North Dakota	3.0–8.5
Florida	5.0	Ohio	4.0–8.0
Georgia	6.0	Oklahoma	4.0
Hawaii	5.85–6.435	Oregon	7.5
Idaho	6.5	Pennsylvania	10.5
Illinois	4.0	Rhode Island	8.0
Indiana	3.0	South Carolina	6.0
Iowa	6.0–10.0	South Dakota	—
Kansas	4.5 (+2.25)*	Tennessee	6.0
Kentucky	4.0–5.8	Texas	—
Louisiana	4.0–8.0	Utah	4.0
Maine	4.95–6.93	Vermont	5.0–7.5
Maryland	7.0	Virginia	6.0
Massachusetts	9.5	Washington	—
Michigan	2.35	West Virginia	6.0
Minnesota	12.0	Wisconsin	2.3–7.9
Mississippi	3.0–4.0	Wyoming	—
Missouri	5.0		

*Surcharge

**A 10 percent surcharge is also imposed.

SOURCE: *All States Tax Handbook,* 1980 (Prentice-Hall). Where a range is given, the state has a progressive income tax. Highest and lowest rates are shown. Federal taxable income is used as a base except in Alabama, Arkansas, California, D.C., Louisiana, Minnesota, Mississippi, Oregon, South Carolina, Utah, and Wisconsin. All or part of federal income tax paid is deductible in Alabama, Arizona, Iowa, Louisiana, Missouri, and North Dakota.

Table 7

State Expenditures for Selected State-Local Functions From Own Revenue Sources, By State, 1977–1978 In Relation to State Personal Income

State	Local Schools	Highways	Welfare	Health and Hospitals
United States	2.24%	0.74%	0.93%[1]	0.74%[1]
Alabama	2.90	1.00	0.44	1.03
Alaska	5.06	1.05	1.24	0.76
Arizona	2.58	0.89	0.38	0.55
Arkansas	2.40	1.30	0.68	0.63
California	1.83	0.40	1.70	0.59
Colorado	2.06	0.51	0.64	0.64
Connecticut	1.34	0.49	0.93	0.70
Delaware	3.63	0.68	0.87	0.70
Florida	2.46	0.56	0.31	0.52
Georgia	2.23	1.08	— *	1.25 *
Hawaii	3.29	0.39	1.52	1.34
Idaho	2.27	1.59	0.66	0.51
Illinois	2.01	0.66	1.29	0.52
Indiana	2.41	0.90	0.32	0.60
Iowa	2.13	1.41	0.86	0.59
Kansas	2.09	0.90	0.80	0.55
Kentucky	2.98	1.80	0.90	0.57
Louisiana	2.85	1.17	0.58	1.07
Maine	2.57	1.13	1.01	0.64
Maryland	2.26	0.81	1.21	0.89
Massachusetts	1.92	0.57	1.85	0.74
Michigan	2.36	0.70	1.33	0.70
Minnesota	3.39	0.94	0.93	0.72
Mississippi	2.64	1.38	0.68	0.85
Missouri	1.54	0.88	0.51	0.63
Montana	3.33	1.20	0.36	0.76
Nebraska	0.89	1.29	0.43	0.67
Nevada	1.52	0.72	0.26	0.45
New Hampshire	0.38	1.13	0.58	0.85
New Jersey	2.05	0.27	0.77	0.56
New Mexico	4.18	1.28	— *	1.04 *
New York	2.25	0.40	0.84	1.06
North Carolina	3.34	1.14	— *	1.04 *
North Dakota	2.33	1.29	0.54	0.63
Ohio	1.73	0.73	0.83	0.73
Oklahoma	2.68	1.02	0.59	0.58
Oregon	1.53	1.02	1.01	0.67
Pennsylvania	2.44	0.70	1.64	0.88
Rhode Island	1.87	0.36	1.70	1.53

(Continued on following page)

Table 7 (cont'd)

State	Local Schools	Highways	Welfare	Health and Hospitals
South Carolina	2.88	0.78	0.61	1.16
South Dakota	0.71	1.19	0.57	0.82
Tennessee	2.12	1.01	0.58	0.63
Texas	2.51	0.64	0.36	0.63
Utah	3.38	0.63	0.65	0.83
Vermont	1.70	0.73	0.83	0.80
Virginia	1.74	1.17	0.54	1.00
Washington	2.72	0.87	1.04	0.43
West Virginia	3.17	1.84	0.63	0.72
Wisconsin	1.94	0.77	1.17	0.73
Wyoming	1.51	1.87	0.24	0.62

*Public welfare expenditures for Georgia, New Mexico, and North Carolina are included with health and hospital expenditures. Data necessary for separations are not available for FY 1978.

SOURCE: Table 21, *Significant Features of Fiscal Federalism, 1979–1980 Edition.* M-123, Advisory Commission on Intergovernmental Relations. Washington, D.C., October 1980.

section will simply identify the direction of reasonably expected effects.

Corporate Net Income Tax

Income taxation of business profits can have incentive effects on the location of investments, the magnitude of investments, and the capital/labor ratio selected. Since income taxes are based on the accounting definition of profits, instead of the economic definition, they are in part a tax on the return to capital and management factors of production. As such, interstate differentials in income tax rates should be expected to reduce the level of investment in high tax states, lower the capital/labor ratio, and reduce the number of projects in high tax states. A state whose sole taxation of business was through an income tax should differentially attract firms which have unstable profits, because they would have no tax liability in bad years—in contrast to states where the principal business tax was a property tax, which applied regardless of income.

Sales Tax

Both the level and the tax base for a sales tax are of interest. If applied to business purchases, a sales tax directly increases the cost of operation. However, in almost all states, business inputs which are used in a manufacturing process are exempted from the sales tax. Naturally, the higher the rate, the larger the potential impact.

Real and Personal Property Taxation   While the property tax is not a major contributor to state revenues in the great majority of states, it is important in a few states, and dominant in many local communities. The important point to understand is that in the short run property taxes fall most heavily on immobile capital. Hence, in a state which taxes real property (land and structures) and personal property (plant and equipment) as well as inventory, the most significant impact will be on land prices and the level and composition of fixed investment. Because of the mobility of inventories, many states have fully or partially exempted inventories from property taxation. Real property taxation is to some degree capitalized in land prices, although there is substantial uncertainty in the empirical literature as to the degree. If land markets were perfect, all land prices would fully reflect property tax differences, so that there would be no geographical incentive effect.

Personal Income Tax   For completeness, it is useful to mention several of the possible incentive effects of personal income taxation. Higher personal tax rates are sometimes thought to lead to interstate migration toward low-tax states, reduced work effort, reduced personal savings, and for unincorporated businesses, a lessened rate of new business formation.

STATE TAX INCENTIVES FOR NEW AND EXPANDING INDUSTRY

States offer a number of tax incentives to new and expanding manufacturers (see Table 8 below for details on two state incentives), where an incentive is a conscious and automatic feature of the tax code, which is conditioned upon a hiring, purchase, or investment decision. As of 1980, the most popular state incentives were sales tax exemptions for raw materials used in production (forty-six states), sales tax exemptions on new equipment (thirty-one states), and a variety of general investment and employment income tax credits (fifteen states).

State corporate income tax credits include both investment and employment tax credits, and a few states combine investment and employment credits. A typical employment credit allows a reduction in state taxes based on some proportion of new wages and salaries. Others condition the credit on personal characteristics of the new employees. (For example, Massachusetts gives tax credits for hiring individuals who were receiving unemployment insurance or public assistance, or were participants in a job training program. Such targeted incentives are excluded from this study.) Investment tax credits are usually based on the value of depreciable investment, with the size of the credit sometimes increasing with the depreciable life of

Table 8

Selected State Tax Incentives for New and Expanding Industry

State	Corporate Income Tax Exemption	Sales Tax Exemption on New Equipment	State	Corporate Income Tax Exemption	Sales Tax Exemption on New Equipment
Alabama		x	Montana	o	
Alaska		x	Nebraska		
Arizona			Nevada		
Arkansas		x	New Hampshire		
California			New Jersey		x
Colorado	o	x	New Mexico	o	
Connecticut			New York	o	x
Delaware	o	x	North Carolina		x
D.C.			North Dakota	o	
Florida		x	Ohio		x
Georgia		x	Oklahoma	o	x
Hawaii			Oregon		x
Idaho		x	Pennsylvania		x
Illinois		x	Rhode Island	o	x
Indiana		x	South Carolina		x
Iowa			South Dakota		
Kansas	o		Tennessee	o	x
Kentucky			Texas		
Louisiana	o	x	Utah		
Maine	o	x	Vermont		x
Maryland		x	Virginia		x
Massachusetts	o	x	Washington		
Michigan		x	West Virginia	o	x
Minnesota			Wisconsin		x
Mississippi		x	Wyoming		
Missouri	o	x			

SOURCE: Compiled from state promotional literature, various issues of *State Tax Review* (Commerce Clearing House), and *Industrial Development*.

the asset. Sales tax exemptions are frequently very narrowly targeted to politically influential industries, but most states also have broad-based incentives applying to all new machinery and equipment intended for expansion, replacement, or new facility.

States have significantly increased their use of these tax incentives since the late 1960s (see Table 9 below). The number of states offering sales tax exemptions for machinery and equipment has gone from eighteen to thirty-one in twelve years, while the number of broad-based income tax credits has increased from none in 1968 to fifteen in 1980. Casual inspection reveals that much of the increased use of these incentives came after the early 1970s. The early 1970s were years in which many state legislatures concentrated on environmental issues, and took a generally skeptical approach to industrial development. The 1974 recession seemed to have dramatically increased the interest of state governments in using all available tools to increase employment and income. However the recent proliferation of tax limitation measures may act to reduce interest in revenue-losing tax incentives.

Table 9

Increased Use of State Tax Incentives

Year in Full Effect	General Investment and Employment Income Tax Credits	Sales Tax Exemptions for New Equipment
1980	15	31
1979	11	31
1978	8	—
1977	7	27
1976	6	27
1975	5	25
1974	5	23
1973	5	25
1972	5	21
1971	4	23
1970	1	23
1969	1	21
1968	0	18

SOURCE: Compiled from state promotional literature, various issues of *State Tax Review* (Commerce Clearing House), and *Industrial Development*.

The particular incentives available vary both in size and in the nature of the base activity eligible for subsidy. Table 10 presents a summary of the general development incentives available at the state level as of December 1980.

While it is extremely easy to determine the availability of specific tax incentives by reference to trade journals and various proprietary tax guides, it is far more difficult to estimate the frequency of their use or the magnitude of the initial revenue loss to state governments. In contrast to the federal government, which is required to publish an annual supplement to the budget in which it estimates the magnitude of tax expenditures in a number of programmatic areas, only three state governments make such estimates. California, Michigan, and Maryland has each published estimates of the tax expenditures in their budgets, although none has state-level industrial tax incentives. Hence, no estimates exist of the recent magnitudes of state revenue losses from various incentives.[1]

All locally exempted property simply does not appear in many records. Similarly, exemptions from sales tax collections are not recorded anywhere. Theoretically, it is possible to determine the claims for employment or investment tax credits on state corporate returns. However, in conducting this study, no state was willing to reveal such figures or allow access to corporate tax returns.

Clearly, a necessary step toward good public policy is to periodically evaluate business tax incentives. One of the reasons that tax incentives can be repeatedly proposed and passed is the general (and specific) lack of evaluations of their effectiveness. For those firms which benefit from tax incentives, and their representatives, it is clearly attractive for tax subsidies to remain an off-budget item, since quantification is a necessary first step toward evaluation. The new research reported in Chapter Four should provide a partial guide to those interested in future and more detailed evaluations.

FOOTNOTES TO CHAPTER 1

[1]In writing this book, the author was initially promised access to state corporate income tax records in a number of states. This cooperation was eventually withdrawn.

Table 10

State General Tax Incentives Designed to Stimulate Manufacturing

State	General Description of Incentive
Colorado	$50 credit per new employee and $50 credit per $100,000 depreciable investment in new or expanded manufacturing facility, available for up to ten years.
Delaware	$75 credit per new employee and $185 credit per $100,000 investment in new or expanded manufacturing facility with at least 25 employees, available for ten years.
Kansas	$50 credit per new employee plus $50 credit per $100,000 investment in a new or expanded manufacturing facility, available for up to ten years.
Louisiana	$100 credit per new employee in a manufacturing facility (larger credits for certain individuals and certain areas). State can also lower taxes to meet lower state taxes offered elsewhere.
Maine	10% credit for depreciable investment. Total investment must be at least $5 million.
Massachusetts	3% credit for depreciable investment in manufacturing facility.
Missouri	$100 credit per new employee plus $100 credit per $100,000 new investment in expanding manufacturing facility. For new plants, parallel credits are at $75.
New Mexico	3.75% credit of value of new machinery and equipment used in manufacturing.
New York	4% credit for depreciable investment in new or expanded manufacturing facility.
Montana	1% credit for wages paid new employees in new or expanding manufacturing facility.
North Dakota	1% credit of wages for new employees in manufacturing facility for first three years, .5% for fourth and fifth years.
Oklahoma	.5% credit for depreciable investment in manufacturing facility which increases employment.
Rhode Island	2% credit for depreciable investment in manufacturing facility.
Tennessee	.2% credit for industrial machinery, increasing to 1.0% after July 1984.
West Virginia	10% credit for depreciable investment with 1% increments available for ten years.

SOURCE: Compiled from promotional literature of various states and issues of *State Tax Review* (Commerce Clearing House)

2

INDUSTRIAL TAX INCENTIVES AS A PUBLIC INVESTMENT

State corporate tax incentives intended to induce additional investment or employment are public investments, and should be analyzed within the framework of a large body of public finance literature. The decision rules for such public investment are well known: the investment should be made if (1) the rate of return on the tax incentive, adjusted for risk, exceeds the social opportunity cost of capital, or equivalently (2) the net present value of the stream of benefits and costs arising from the investment is positive. Additional public investments can be justified until the last dollar of subsidy has a return just equal to the cost of capital and the net present value is zero.

These principles are well known among economists, but somewhat obscure among development officials and elected representatives. Rather than develop a full discussion of public investment rules, this paper will serve simply to highlight some issues of particular concern to tax incentives: (1) the key question of uncertainty about the effect of the subsidy; (2) the difference between automatic subsidies and negotiated subsidies; and (3) the different costs and benefits taken into account by a private firm, a state development official, and a national observer.

THE IMPACT OF UNCERTAINTY ON THE PUBLIC INVESTMENT DECISION

The public investment decision should count only the costs and benefits resulting from investment or employment which would not have occurred without the tax subsidy. All other investment or hiring decisions should be excluded from consideration. There is an unfortunate tendency among some advocates of state tax incentives to assume that all businesses which receive a subsidy on the basis of an investment or hiring decision would not have done so in its absence. In some cases, the investment or hiring would have taken place, but at a lesser volume or level. In others, the investment or hiring would not have taken place at all. Any public investment or social benefit-cost analysis must make some judgment about the sensitivity of investment or hiring with respect to the subsidy. Alternatively, some estimate of the proportion of subsidized investment or hiring which would not have taken place in the absence of the subsidy can be used. While many local property tax incentives *21* are discretionary, meaning local officials can bargain with company representatives over the existence, depth, and length of property tax abatements, most state tax incentives are automatic. All a firm must do, if it has made an investment or hired new workers, is fill out a form, and it will automatically receive the tax credit. Because the state does not seek to determine, at the time of the tax credit, whether or not the investment would have been made in any case, the state faces uncertainty in that it does not know the true effect of the incentives. This is true uncertainty, where not even the proportion of investment affected is known, as opposed to risk, in which the proportion is known, but there is uncertainty about which specific investments make up the affected proportion.

The state also bears uncertainty with respect to the magnitude of benefits and costs for those firms which are actually induced to invest or hire more. Just as an equity investor in a business faces risk with respect to the future profitability of the firm, the public investor's return will depend on the future growth, profitability, and employment of the subsidized business. Similarly, as will become clear below, the state cannot know with certainty the extent to which the employment generated by a project will benefit in-state residents, the previously unemployed, or out-of-state residents. Some of this risk can be diversified by the public investor through the portfolio effects of subsidizing a large number of companies, some of which will succeed and others fail. However, the state cannot diversify away the effects of business cycles (and does not have access to future markets to diversify across time).

These distinctions between uncertainty and risk, and diversifiable and undiversifiable risk, should directly influence the public investment decision. As discussed above, the decision to invest is based in part on the required rate of return (or opportunity cost of capital). A great deal of literature and experience in financial markets states that a major investor, with investments in a diversified portfolio, should be much less concerned about risk than a small investor with an undiversified portfolio (see Daniels and Kieschnick, 1979 for more on this point). If the state views its collection of individual tax incentives to specific firms as an investment portfolio, what rate of return should it require? Clearly the state is a "large investor," and will have a diversified portfolio—at least among manufacturing firms within the state. However, even a large public investor should be concerned about true uncertainty—not knowing even a guess about the effectiveness of its incentives—and business cycle risk. Accordingly, the state should seek a higher return on its "portfolio" of incentives than it would if it were investing in low-risk Treasury bills.

THE INFLUENCE OF AUTOMATIC VERSUS NEGOTIATED SUBSIDIES

Traditional investment decision rules call for making incremental investments until the last dollar of investment has a marginal net return of zero. At that point, the net benefits of the program (or net development impact) will be maximized.

To carry out such a decision rule, however, the investor (whether public or private) must face a schedule of independent investment opportunities, each with an associated expected rate of return. With no constraint on the amount invested, the investor simply invests in projects in order of return until the next project has an unacceptable rate of return.

If state tax incentives are provided on the basis of negotiations between public developers with a subsidy fund and a set of private firms, this underlying picture has a great deal of relevance. Based on the results of the negotiations about level of subsidy, investment and hiring practices, and public services to be provided, the public investor would simply invest in all those projects whose expected return was sufficient. Marginal decision rules could be used. Of course, factors other than public benefit may enter into negotiations, as political figures, consultants, and "deal packagers" seek to influence the subsidy decision.

However, the great majority of state tax incentives are provided automatically, rather than through negotiations. So long as a firm meets certain criteria, and actually makes the investment or hires an additional employee, the tax incentive is provided. No assessment of the expected return on each project is made. In this case, the decision to provide public subsidies is an all-or-none (lumpy and discontinuous) decision. Legislators or elected officials must make the decision to implement a subsidy program based on an assessment of the average return and must assume that the marginal decision rule will be violated. It is impossible to predict whether or not the tendency would be to overinvest or underinvest (thus foregoing valuable investments).

DIFFERING PERSPECTIVES OF THE FIRM, A STATE, AND SOCIETY

The evaluation of an investment opportunity will be critically influenced by which costs and benefits are counted. In many situations, a private firm, a state government, and society as a whole would make different decisions about the same investment project because they include or ignore different benefits and cost.

From the point of view of a private business, only direct revenues and costs are included in the calculation of a net profit estimate. The existence of a tax incentive will alter the net profits of a given investment by reducing the tax costs in a given state. This may make a previously unacceptable investment acceptable, or may simply increase the profitability of an already chosen investment opportunity. However, the private firm is not interested in whether or not personal income in the state of its choice is increased or decreased, or who obtains any new jobs, or whether or not the tax incentive made a difference in the location decision—so long as it does reduce costs.

A single state government should incorporate different costs and benefits into its decisionmaking process. The benefits to the state include net increases in income due to induced investment or hiring, reduced welfare or transfer payment costs, and any increased tax revenues from the expanded economic activity. If the tax incentive does not induce greater investment or hiring, there are no net benefits to the state although there will be to the private firm. The costs to the state include the revenue initially foregone through the subsidy to all subsidized investments or hirings—not just those which are changed—and any increased public service costs or new infrastructure required by induced investments and hirings.

From the point of view of a single state, investments which are merely shifted from one state to another count as much as those investments which would have occurred in no location without the subsidy. A somewhat more difficult conceptual question arises in determining whether or not to count wages and salaries paid to workers who are brought in from out of state to work in induced projects. Such wages and salaries provide no direct benefits to the then current voters/citizens of the state where the subsidy decision (whether automatic or negotiated) was made. At a minimum, there are important distributional questions if a tax subsidy is borne by initial residents while the benefits are borne in part by immigrants.

If a state maintains its level of services (and hence budget) while providing tax incentives, the taxes borne elsewhere must increase. The losses sustained by other taxpayers to compensate merely represent a transfer from those subsidized to those paying higher taxes. In this case, there is no direct tax loss to the state. The benefit-cost decision then must be determined on the basis of relative induced changes in economic activity due to the changed composition of taxes.

This relative incentive effect is illustrated in Figure I below. Consider a state which has two classes of firms—stable (those which are not considering expanding, locating, or leaving the state) and marginal (those which are considering investment decisions). With a uniform tax rate on corporate income, and investment demand equations which are a function of the after-tax cost of capital $s+t$, the stable firms will invest $\bar{I}_2$ and the unstable firms will invest I_2. In each case, the mere existence of taxes, assuming some elasticity of investment with respect to taxation, means that investment is foregone. For the stable firms, the lost investment is equal to $\bar{I}_1 - \bar{I}_2$, where $\bar{I}_1$ is the amount which would have been invested with no taxation of capital.

For unstable firms, the lost investment is $I_1 - I_2$, where I_2 is the amount which would have been invested with no taxation. If the state introduces a tax incentive by placing no taxes on the marginal firm, and shifts them all to the stable firm (in that ideal world in which the firms could be so identified), the relative incentive effects must be compared. So the stable firms must pay a cost of capital of $s+t'$ while the unstable firms have a cost of capital equal only to s. Now, given the demand curves, an additional amount of investment is lost in the stable firms, equal to $\bar{I}_3 - \bar{I}_2$, while investment in unstable firms is increased by $I_1 - I_2$. If the increased investment exceeds the reduced investment, the state is better off (assuming away, for the moment, the other costs involved). If the increased investment from marginal firms is less than the reduced investment from stable firms, the state is worse off for shifting taxes. This indicates the importance of accurately targeting incentive policies not only in lowering taxes for firms with elastic investment responses, but in raising them (or perhaps reducing services) for those with inelastic investment responses.

Figure 1

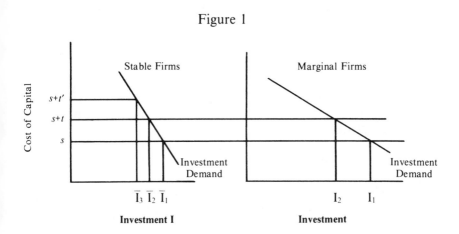

A true social cost-benefit decision is indifferent to the location of the investment. Thus, if investment is simply shifted in location, but not in amount, the result is no net increase in economic welfare. Only if the tax incentive serves to correct labor market failures, which will be discussed in more detail in a following section, can the zero-sum investment outcome produce increased net benefits. For the most part, a social analysis of tax incentives will thus count only the incremental investment at the national level. This will result in reducing the percent of investments having received subsidies which will be counted as *25*

benefits, because those which merely shift location are eliminated. However, since the social analysis is also indifferent to the previous residence of newly hired workers, it will not eliminate in-migrants to a state from the benefit side. Thus, a larger proportion of the wages and salaries for those investments which are induced will be counted. Most analysts believe that the reduction in the share of investment counted outweighs the increase in wages and salaries counted for each induced investment, thus lowering the attractiveness of state incentives when evaluated at a national level.

When an incentive to one firm, or one class of firms, is offset by increases in taxes to another class of firms, the benefits depend on the relative incentive effects, just as in the single state analysis. In terms of the graphical presentation, the elasticity of investment with respect to state taxes becomes smaller when viewed from the national perspective.

COMPETING JUSTIFICATIONS FOR TAX INCENTIVES

When considered from the perspective of a single state, a review of the voluminous arguments in the academic, political, and business press suggests five different justifications for state tax incentives for investment or employment:

1. equalizing interstate tax differentials, which may serve as an inducement for a firm to select an alternative business location;
2. serving as a wage subsidy to offset the effects of wage rigidity or labor immobility;
3. lowering the cost of capital to induce greater overall capital formation, independent of location choices;
4. serving to redistribute income from labor to capital under the politically acceptable guise of providing development incentives; and
5. serving as a "signal" to out-of-state businesses that the state has generally "pro-business" regulatory and spending policies.

Equalizing Interstate Tax Differentials

All other things being equal, a rational firm with perfect foresight and operating in perfect markets will prefer to produce in states with the best combination of taxes and business services. If possible, a firm will avoid states in which it perceives that its tax burden exceeds the value of services provided, and seek those where value exceeds the tax burden. A relatively tiny percentage of taxes are on a user charge or fee for service basis, so that there is generally little direct connection between revenue sources and service funding.

26   Unfortunately, there is little relevant evidence to indicate whether

state-provided services in general are typically higher or lower in value than state-imposed taxes. It is perfectly possible that all states presently provide businesses with services whose value exceeds the tax burden (or the converse). All of the empirical work dealing with the issue of the fiscal impact of new industrial development has been concerned with local impacts (for a good review of this literature, see Reigeluth, et al., 1979). The literature, while quite mixed in quality, indicates that there is a wide variety of experience, with some specific projects providing significant surpluses and others requiring significant subsidies. The result depends not only on the existence of tax subsidies for the firm, but on whether or not the firm's labor force requires the construction of new infrastructure. Naturally, the provision of tax subsidies reduces the likelihood of a fiscal surplus, and the use of an underutilized local labor force increases the likelihood of a fiscal surplus. Since state business taxes are not precisely (and could not be) on a fee for service basis, there will always be some firms with above average service needs with a lower than average tax "price" for services and some firms with a higher than average tax "price" for services. Unless tax incentives are negotiated, they cannot be used to selectively provide reductions to firms facing higher than average tax prices, if such firms can be identified.

The provision of selective income tax credits based on new investment or employment is usually seen as a less costly alternative to general business tax reductions. Reductions are offered only to those firms actually considering an action which might create new income. A general reduction in business taxes sufficient to influence this limited number of firms to the same degree would be far more costly to the state because of the windfalls to firms not considering investment or employment decisions.

The value of the attempt to increase economic activity by equalizing "price" differentials depends critically on the elasticity of the investment or employment response to the subsidy. The larger the proportion which are actually influenced, and the larger the average size of their reaction, the higher the return on the state public investment. There is a significant body of literature addressing the relative influence of different factors—including taxes—on the industrial location decision, which will be reviewed in the next chapter.

Offsetting Labor Market Failures

The wage rigidity and labor immobility arguments have been made most forcefully by Moes (1961) and Rinehart and Laird (1972). They argue that the existence of unemployment in a community indicates that wages are insufficiently flexible for workers unwilling to move to areas with job openings. That is, local wage rates are too high relative to the marginal productivity of labor given the relevant capital/labor ratio and other cost factors in an area. They argue that tax policy is frequently the only public policy to offset "high" wages. Many of these arguments were developed before the increasingly prevalent set of alternative labor market policies seen in the 1970s: training to upgrade skills (which might be seen as increasing the value of workers relative to "high" wages), job placement programs to better match workers with available jobs (which serves to help workers break out of "informal" networks of information about job openings), and relocation subsidies, by which workers can be induced to relocate from depressed areas into growing areas. Where tax subsidies are used to offset wage rigidities, they should be well targeted to only those workers whose labor market value is less than their wages, with the upper limit on the subsidies equal to the difference between wages and market value.

Both authors generally address the practice of local property taxes, rather than state subsidies. They suggest that only communities with unemployment will offer subsidies. The degree of competition among communities and the magnitude of the unemployment problem will determine the level of subsidy. They assert that the present level of local subsidy is too low (since unemployment remains), and suggest that if competitive subsidization were allowed to take its full course, equilibrium would occur when all communities are at full employment.

These arguments rely heavily on investors shifting their desired capital/labor ratio in response to wage subsidies. If the capital/labor ratio was relatively constant among locations, wage subsidies which were successful in influencing the location of investment would simply redistribute unemployment, rather than increase overall employment.

Buchanan and Moes (1962) have suggested that newly employed workers be subject to an "income-added" tax to provide subsidies to new and expanding firms. Under some circumstances, the subsidies involved in such a scheme could be quite large. For example, consider the case of a town with 100 unemployed workers, each completely unwilling to relocate. A firm is considering locating in the town and offering employment to these workers, but has forced them to compete with other communities in offering subsidies. The jobs available offer salaries of $10,000 per year and will be available indefinitely (that is, there is no threat of failure or relocation). If workers consider such income as the return on an investment from a subsidy, and their alternative investment opportunities return 10 percent per year, what will each worker be willing to offer as a subsidy? Under extreme competition, and placing no value on leisure, the workers would be willing to bid up to about $100,000 per job in an up-front subsidy. No state presently offers subsidies of anywhere near this magnitude (for reasons to be discussed below).

Lowering the Cost of There is now substantial discussion about
Capital To Increase the appropriate national tax policy to
Investment induce additional corporate investment in
fixed structures, plant, and equipment. This
reflects considerable uncertainty about the influence of tax policy on
the level (as distinct from the location) of investment. If, as argued by
some economists, the "wedge" between private and public return on
investment caused by taxation of business income causes capital to
flow into less taxed areas or consumption, it is also possible that
reductions in the level of state taxation of business income will increase
investment. Corresponding to this "income" effect due to reduced
income taxation is the "substitution" effect of simply reducing the
labor content of production and increasing the capital content due to
the investment tax credit. There is no consensus as to the relative
importance of the two effects at the national level, and little study of
the issue at the state level.

There are two possible ways in which lowering the taxes on capital
income might influence the amount of investment without changing
the capital/labor ratio. First, a firm may simply decide that additional
production can be justified at the lower tax rates, and add an
additional machine, assembly line, or structure to expand output.
Because state corporate income taxes are substantially lower than
federal income taxes, the level of additional justifiable output is likely
to be quite small. Unless small increments of output are easily matched
with small amounts of new capital (i.e., investment plans of
corporations would have to be quite "divisible" at the margin), it is
unlikely that small incentives would influence the amount (as opposed
to the location) of investment. Alternatively, the increased cash flow
due to lowered taxes may not have any influence on the project which
generates the tax incentive, but may make possible an additional
investment at some other location or time.

Using Tax Incentives Some observers, notably Kanter (1977)
to Redistribute Income and Harrison and Kanter (1978), focus on
from Capital to Labor the effects of state tax incentives on
functional distribution of income. They
note the near consensus of surveys of business decision-makers that
taxes and tax incentives have very little influence on location or
investment decisions at the state level. Yet, under the influence of
business arguments that tax relief will increase employment (or reduce
employment losses), legislators continue to offer additional incentives.
They argue that tax incentives, wrapped in the politically palatable
guise of job creation, merely serve as an acceptable way to increase the
share of income going to capital. The argument does not particularly
depend on the motivations of legislators, who could simply believe the ***29***

claims of business representatives. *If* tax incentives have little or no influence on corporate behavior, the validity of the Kanter/Harrison argument depends crucially on the incidence of state taxes on corporate income. Kanter and Harrison assume that such taxes fall solely on shareholders. As noted above, there is nothing approaching a consensus on this issue. Given the debate in this area, it is equally possible to argue that the tax incentives provide relief to consumers, in the absence of any effect on investment or employment.

Tax Incentives as a "Signal" to Out-of-State Investors

A final justification frequently asserted by development practitioners is that while tax incentives do not offer cost savings sufficient to affect corporate decisions, they do serve as a signaling device of the "business climate" in a state. This argument focuses on the psychological aspects of corporate decisions, as well as on the cost to the firm of obtaining accurate information about public services, regulations, political attitudes, and future tax levels. Because of these costs, and because businessmen enjoy public attention, states find that tax incentives are an inexpensive way to signal firms of a state's interest in development. From the point of view of firms, it is far easier to check on the existence of tax incentives through the quick perusal of easily obtainable tax guides or industrial development publications than to examine in detail the attributes of each potential location. This argument offers a plausible justification for the proliferation of a large number of tax incentives whose value to a firm, in terms of percentage of investment or wage bill covered, is extraordinarily low. The primary weakness of the argument is that it is similarly inexpensive for other states, with less attractive attributes, to offer inexpensive incentives as well. If a competitive environment exists, other states would rapidly have to offer larger incentives or provide nontax signals. In general, it appears that nontax signals have been the favored response, as state recruiting teams have become increasingly important in providing direct contact with industrial prospects.

THE EFFECT OF THE DISTRIBUTION OF BENEFITS AND COSTS ON THE PUBLIC INVESTMENT DECISION

Since automatic tax incentives must be approved by the state legislative body and governor, their presence indicates at least majority legislative approval, if not popular approval, for their use. Leaving aside the use of tax incentives to redistribute income directly, legislators and governors must believe that the rate of return on the investment is higher than the opportunity cost (recognizing that it is unlikely to be thought of or analyzed in this way). However, of a least equal importance as the expected rate of return is the expected distribution of benefits and costs.

The actual public investment decision is determined by the interaction between the political structure of the state, the fiscal structure, and the distribution of benefits and costs. If the distribution of benefits and costs are quite unequal, the fiscal structure and the political structure of the state must serve to redistribute costs and benefits. If not redistributed, even subsidies with a very high expected rate of return will face major political obstacles in passage.

Vaughan (1980) has suggested that elected bodies, in the aftermath of Abscam, be selected in a competitive bidding process. Each person running for office would offer his/her proposals for bid by competing interests, with the person receiving the largest dollar amount of bids winning. Thus, with a tax incentive proposal to be considered in the next legislative session, all voters would consider the likely distribution of costs and benefits to themselves, taking into account the effects of lost or altered revenues, the new jobs, the effects on suppliers, and similar direct and indirect effects. Each voter would then tender bids to candidates supporting or opposing the proposal based on their position on the tax subsidy. If a number of conditions are met, proposals with net benefits will win, and those with net losses will lose. The most important of these conditions are:

1. accurate information about the magnitude and incidence of costs and benefits;
2. perfect capital markets so that those who might gain benefits after a tax subsidy but who are without assets or income before the subsidy can borrow funds for bidding; and
3. separation of each issue facing the legislature from all others in the voting (bidding) process.

Clearly these conditions are not met. The existence of this study indicates that the first condition is not met. Capital markets are clearly inefficient for those without current assets or income. Candidates for office must offer positions on a variety of issues, which are then inseparable in voting.

When elections are not conducted in this manner (and they are not), and these conditions are not met, the political process substitutes other mechanisms to transform an expected return on public subsidies into votes for and against the proposal. For the most part, tax incentives are not widely discussed, and are rarely issues in a majority of the legislators' election campaigns. Thus, legislators are dependent upon lobbying, legislative research, and their own beliefs about the likely rate of return.

The interaction of these factors determines whether or not the subsidies offered (and not offered) are insufficient or overly generous. Particularly in the absence of accurate information about the expected rate of return, the relative political strength of those who expect to gain (typically businesses) and those who expect to lose (typically taxpayer organizations, social service beneficiaries, and unions) through offsetting taxes or program cuts in the legislature determines the existence, magnitude, and targeting of incentives.

With most tax incentives, the costs (increased offsetting taxes or program cuts) are more diffuse than the benefits (lower tax bills for some firms and increased employment in some cases). This should impart a bias toward greater subsidies if concentration increases the ability to organize political support. On the other hand, the failure of most state and local tax systems to capture many of the benefits and redistribute some portion of them to those who face net costs will result in greater political obstacles. The political obstacles increase as the distribution of costs and benefits becomes more unequal. Thus, it is impossible to predict in general whether the political process produces a bias toward or against subsidies without knowing the specific tax system and political structure of each state.

POSSIBLE NATIONAL JUSTIFICATION FOR STATE TAX INCENTIVES

The previous section considered possible justifications for instituting state tax incentives when viewed solely from the perspective of a single state. This section attempts to determine the conditions under which state tax incentives will result in an increase in national benefits. The primary basis of the discussion is viewing the use of state tax incentives as a competitive game among states, with tax structures the primary method of competition.

Following Rinehart and Laird (1972), the game starts in some state with unemployment due to wage rigidity or labor immobility. Only in such areas will there be a positive return to tax incentives. With subsidies, additional investment will occur in labor-surplus regions, with capital/labor ratios for the incremental investment being lower than in other areas. Thus, the redistribution of incremental investment creates additional national employment.

The game continues when another state with its own excess labor pool observes the success of the first state in creating new employment (perhaps achieved in part by attracting firms which would have located in the second state). The entry of the second firm into the game, by offering competing incentives, lowers the initial advantage of the first state. The process continues, with other states adding incentives (thereby entering the game) so long as the value of the new employment they expect to be generated exceeds the loss of tax revenues from the initial subsidy. The competitive process should go through an unending series of maneuvers, reflecting the changing balance as each new state enters and as national factors influence relative unemployment rates among states. In theory, the process should continually move states toward full employment situations, thereby providing overall national benefits along with benefits for each state.

Factors Limiting the Process of Competitive Subsidization

Casual observation indicates that not all states with unemployment offer tax incentives, and those states with tax incentives continue to have unemployment. Either the process of competitive subsidization never reaches equilibrium because of continually changing macroeconomic conditions (as discussed above), or firms do not respond to incentives as assumed, or information and structural problems limit the competitive process.

There are two major instances when the competitive process does not work simply because firms do not react as assumed. In the first case, firms may change their location but not their capital/labor ratios. In this situation, competitive subsidization is a zero-sum game, with investment and employment merely shifted from one location to another. Many opponents of state tax incentives consider this to be what usually occurs. In the second case, few if any firms react at all, simply accepting the reduced taxes without changing their behavior. Thus, employment and investment is not shifted, only the tax burden is altered.

If subsidized firms do react as assumed, there are a number of factors which should serve to limit the competitive process. Among the most important are the lack of adequate information, inadequate transfer mechanisms, the effect of increased taxes on other sectors of the economy, and political concerns over equity in the structure of tax systems. Lack of adequate information will occur whenever businesses are unaware of incentives or legislators are unaware of their asserted benefits. Inadequate transfer mechanisms refer simply to the difficulty in obtaining political support for subsidies to selected firms when there is a distinct possibility that they will be raised for other firms or for individuals. As discussed above in reference to the targeting of incentives to responsive firms, if the incentives result in additional taxes on firms or individuals who are sensitive to higher taxes, the benefits of the initial subsidies may simply be canceled out. These firms or individuals may hire fewer people or spend less, thereby offsetting any additional hiring in the originally subsidized firms. Finally, in addition to these economic arguments, there frequently exists political opposition to tax incentives based solely on standards of fairness in the design of tax systems.

There currently exists strong political and analytical disagreement over the likely rate of return on tax incentives, the distribution of any benefits and their certain costs, and their fairness to nonsubsidized firms and individuals. When these disagreements are coupled with significant problems in transferring benefits from those subsidized to those not subsidized through the tax system, and political systems which do not act on Vaughan's Abscam model but on frequently more random methods, it is quite clear that "market" for state tax incentives is quite inefficient. However, it is impossible to predict whether or not the net effect of the inefficiencies is that too many incentives exist or too few.

3

A REVIEW OF THE EMPIRICAL LITERATURE

A theoretical discussion of the effect of state tax incentives is insufficient to guide decisionmakers in choices about whether or not to institute, amend, or repeal such incentives. Further empirical information is required to make sensible development policy.

From a policy perspective, it would be valuable to have answers to the following empirical questions:

1. What is the relevant weight of state and local business taxes compared to such factors as wages?
2. How much do state and local taxes on business vary between states?
3. What is the current level of state tax expenditures in support of industrial development?
4. What types of firms are receiving which types of tax expenditures?
5. What is the elasticity of investment with respect to state taxation of business?
6. What proportion of firms considering investment are aware of state tax incentives?
7. What proportion of firms considering investment seriously consider locating in another state?
8. Is the primary effect of state tax incentives on the location or the amount of investment?
9. What is the expected rate of return on state tax incentives?

A number of these questions do not appear to have been asked in previous studies. In particular, there have been no estimates of the current level of state tax expenditures, the types of firms receiving tax incentives, the proportion of firms aware of the incentives, the proportion of firms choosing among states for a new investment, or the relative effect of tax incentives on location and the amount of investment. The remaining questions have been addressed in at least one study, but the conclusions are generally limited to a few states or are flawed by the research methodology.

This chapter will primarily review the existing empirical literature. Ideally, the empirical literature should be shaped by underlying theoretical considerations. The key theoretical issues relate to the methods by which firms make the location portion of an investment decision, so a brief section will review several frequently neglected aspects of the location decision. Following this discussion, the chapter will review studies in five different areas:

1. studies reviewing different methods of measuring the business tax burden;
2. studies attempting to determine the relative share of state and local business taxes on business scales or profits and compare that share to other factors such as wages;
3. studies using surveys and interviews with business decisionmakers to evaluate the relative importance of different factors thought to influence the manufacturing location decision;
4. studies using statistical techniques to determine the relative importance of tax differentials in the manufacturing location decision; and
5. studies using case studies to evaluate the rate of return on particular firms' receipt of state tax incentives.

SELECTED THEORETICAL ASPECTS OF THE BUSINESS INVESTMENT DECISION

In the simplest neoclassical approach to investment, a firm faces a schedule of independent investments, each with known costs and revenues. Under competitive markets (including capital markets), a firm will undertake all investments in which the discounted cash flow is positive at the after-tax cost of capital. When a firm faces revenues and costs which are certain but vary spatially, under similar circumstances it will undertake each investment whose return exceeds the cost of capital. Where a firm faces some discontinuity in the availability of capital, or lacks management capacity to undertake all investments of acceptable return, it will choose investments in order of return.

Search Costs

An important qualification to these models of business investment and location behavior is that information about prices, markets, and costs is costly for both the present and future. This costly process of acquiring information will directly affect location decisions. A profit maximizing process of investment decisionmaking requires accurate information about each project at each possible location. If the costs of search increase less than proportionately to project size, firms undertaking smaller projects could be expected to search less than those undertaking larger projects. Similarly, since information obtained in a search for new locations by a multiplant firm can be used by units other than the prospective venture, we should expect multiunit firms, controlled for size, to search more widely than single-unit firms. This type of behavior has been confirmed in survey research by Oster (1979). It implies that many firms will not be located at the site of least-cost production excluding search costs. Further, the existence of search costs helps to explain the observation that the great majority of relocations of firms are within a relatively short radius of the prior location (see Schmenner (1978), Wolman (1979), and Jusenius and Ledebur (1977)).

The Effect of Uncertainty

Firms which expect their operations to last for more than a short period of time and having a discount rate of less than infinity will be concerned about future as well as present costs and demand. At some expenditure, uncertainty about present costs can be reduced to a low level. However, most future costs are uncertain with any degree of search (although contracts can be used to reduce uncertainty). Presumably, firms use some conceptual model to predict future prices and costs, which incorporates present trends as well as the effects of their own investment and hiring decisions on markets.

A project with net revenues that are less certain at one location than another (but with the same expected level) will have a higher cost of capital at the less certain location. It is likely that most firms feel more confident (i.e., have more information at a lower level of search costs) at present locations than at distant alternative locations which may be less costly. This aspect of uncertain futures, when added to the cost of search for present information, leads to a potentially large bias to expansion at present sites for existing firms and for new firms to be started in areas familiar to the entrepreneur. Willingness to search and choose new locations over existing ones should increase with company and venture size, as returns to scale are realized.

Several State Location Searches

One method used by firms to reduce search costs is to make location decisions in several stages. Surveys and interviews with business decisionmakers indicate that most large firms tend to select a location in at least two states (see McMillan (1969), and Vaughan (1977)). A region (perhaps a state or larger) is first selected on the basis of such factors as the size of the potential market, the general level of labor costs, or the existence of a reliable supply of a natural resource. Within that region, a number of communities will be examined in much greater detail, with specific information collected on the cost and availability of different types of labor, land, transportation, taxes, and other spatially varying factors. This sort of two-stage process clearly reduces the amount of costly information that would be required relative to a full investigation of all sites, including those in areas that could be eliminated in the first round and   *37* those that are comparable to the sites in the selected region, but aren't worth the cost of a two-region search.

Implications for ***Empirical Research*** These considerations indicate that empirical investigations should, where possible, differentiate between firms which are start-ups, expansions, and new branch plants. In addition, the relative influence of tax burdens may vary at different stages of the location choice—hence, surveys should clearly specify the level of location choice being examined.

TECHNIQUES OF MEASURING DIFFERENCES AMONG STATE TAX BURDENS

"The measurement of comparative state and local tax burdens constitutes one of the more formidable if not wholly intractable tasks in the field of public finance. This is usually recognized by students of taxation despite the fact that special tax committees, industrial development agencies, and representatives of business and sundry other special interest groups are continually "proving" that the tax burdens in their respective states or communities are either higher or lower than those prevailing elsewhere."

So began a piece which appeared in 1961 (Zubrow, 1961). For the most part, relatively little progress has been made in developing a measure agreed upon by economists. This has not slowed the proliferation of comparative and econometric studies relying upon one measure or another.

The most typical methods of comparing state tax burdens for the past two decades has been to compare state and local taxes per capita or per $1,000 personal income using all state and local taxes, or to construct "hypothetical corporations," which are then subjected to prevailing state and local tax rates. Each of these methods overlooks major difficulties if a measure is to be used as representative of the tax burden faced by a firm considering a location choice. The major problems to be considered are those of incidence, offsetting levels of benefits, excessive levels of aggregation, assumptions of factor proportions, temporal variations in taxes, and fiscal interactions among states for firms which do business in more than one state. These problems are considered in order below.

We have previously noted that the signer of the check to the state Department of Finance is not necessarily the party which actually bears the costs of taxes. If a firm was able to pass along all tax costs to workers through lower wages and to consumers through higher prices, it would be indifferent to its tax burden and no measure of tax burden would be relevant to a location choice. For the firm whose shareholders absorbed all of the tax burden, the relevant measure is the taxes actually paid by the corporation facing the location choice. If the tax burden is partially shifted to workers or consumers, the effect of the tax is to reduce effective wages or demand in other sectors, and a broader measure of tax burden is required. While never explicitly stated, an agnostic assumption on incidence of state and local taxes might justify a broad measure of the tax burden, such as state and local taxes per capita or per $1,000 of personal income. Unfortunately, individual taxes within the state and local tax structure are certain to have varying patterns of incidence. For example, the property tax can be separated into a national average tax and local variations, each with separate patterns of incidence. Severance taxes on coal or oil clearly have different patterns of incidence than personal income taxes. The sales tax in a state like Nevada, which is heavily dependent on out-of-state visitors, will be more readily "exported" to nonlocal taxpayers than in most states. All of these factors severely complicate the task of constructing an appropriate measure of tax burden.

As previously discussed, there is at least some relationship between the level of taxes and the level of public services provided. This relationship is affected by the presence of economies of scale, relative wage levels among public jurisdictions, relative levels of efficiency, the mix of public expenditures among those which provide direct benefits and those which are primarily redistributive in nature, and such factors as weather and the influence of the state's congressional delegation in obtaining federal services and grants. No one has yet devised an appropriate measure of the benefits rendered to a business by location, sector, or taxes paid. Under some circumstances, it is equally likely that a high tax state which efficiently provided services with little redistributive spending would be more attractive than a low tax state with few benefits.

One of the most important drawbacks to the use of tax measures based on "hypothetical" firms is that they necessarily obscure many differences among individual firms. What is typically done is to use publicly available figures for the total balance sheets and income statements of different categories of manufacturing firms to construct average balance sheet and income statements. Average state and local tax rates are then applied to the average financial statements to obtain average tax burdens, which are then compared among states. Such studies necessarily assume away much of the diversity among business firms in profitability and composition of taxable assets. The distortion which results from the use of average figures clearly diminishes if less-aggregated types of firms are used in the calculations. Thus, there is likely to be less variation if electronics firms were compared with other electronics firms in terms of profitability and types of assets than there would be if electronics firms were combined in a category with steel mills. A second form of aggregation which leads to some   *39* distortions is the use of average state and local tax rates. Differences do exist among communities within a state in terms of local property tax rates, and such differences are lost in the process of developing an average tax burden for the entire state. Finally, in those states which have graduated corporate income taxes, lumping firms of the same size together, even within the same industry, will mean that the measure of taxes overestimates the taxes actually faced by small firms and underestimates it for large firms. Clearly, subject to data constraints (which are quite severe in most cases), more detailed categories of businesses are preferable to more aggregated categories.

The taxes paid by a corporation may vary substantially over time even if the tax rates on businesses remain unchanged. If the relative proportion of business profits and assets changes over time—perhaps as a new firm or new plant is built and comes into profitable operation—a state with both property taxes and income taxes will levy a changing stream of taxes. Most hypothetical tax comparisons, by selecting an average corporation, implicitly use a comparison of firms at one point in time. It is at least conceivable that firms place widely varying emphasis on the relative tax rates at different periods in the business life-cycle. For example, a high income tax rate will cause little burden to a firm in its initial unprofitable years, while high property taxes could cause substantial harm. In contrast, as the firm becomes quite profitable, the property taxes may become less important, but high income tax rates could be seen as a substantial obstacle.

The primary use of measures of interstate tax burdens is to determine the relative importance of state and local taxes in the business location decision. The use of hypothetical firms to measure tax burdens assumes that it is reasonable to place the same firm in all fifty states, without changing the relative proportions of labor, land, or depreciable assets. Ironically, if businesses actually believe state and local taxes to be important, they may change not only their location but their composition of assets and their capital/labor ratio to minimize tax liabilities once a location is chosen. In fact, in one state a firm may choose to use fewer machines but more workers due to the ratio of taxes on capital to wage costs, while in another it may purchase less land but put more capital into plant and equipment because of the differing assessment ratios on types of property. This factor has not been studied, and it is very difficult to obtain detail at the level of the individual firm to carry out such a study. In the meantime, all methods currently available to compare states implicitly assume that a firm does not change its factor proportions.

Finally, there exists interaction among the fiscal systems of each state. Vasquez and deSave (1977) have stated that the "particular distribution of a firm's existing activities among states and localities can have such a dramatic effect on its after-tax rate of return on marginal investments that broad generalizations about the fiscal interaction of jurisdictions may be impossible to make." This is because of variations in the way in which states use the distribution of sales, assets, and employment to determine taxable income. Vasquez and deSave argue that to truly understand the tax effects of a particular location, knowledge is required of the *present* distribution of plants, employees, and the distribution of sales. However, their argument is weakened by the lack of any evidence that corporate decision-makers understand the implications of interstate taxation practices. A reasonably exhaustive review of the literature generally available to businesses from private sources did not turn up awareness of the issue or proposed responses to it. Nonetheless, an interesting result of the research of Vasquez and deSave, not mentioned in their prose but clear in their empirical results, is that the marginal return may vary somewhat among investments as the pattern of existing activity is altered, but the *ranking* of states is quite stable. It thus may be more appropriate to use the ranking of states to compare different locations rather than to use the single estimate of taxes paid derived from hypothetical firms.

A REPRESENTATIVE SAMPLE OF INTERSTATE TAX COMPARISONS Having reviewed the limitations of interstate tax comparisons, it is still possible to gain some indication of the order of magnitude of interstate tax differentials by examining a small number of studies done as part of state development efforts. In particular, several studies have attempted to relate the magnitude of interstate tax differentials to wage differences or total operating cost differences. A recent example of the hypothetical firm method of calculating state business tax burdens is furnished in a study performed by the major accounting firm Price Waterhouse under contract to the State of Missouri in 1978 (see Table 11). The state furnished Price Waterhouse with balance sheet and income statements, as well as other operating assumptions, for a "typical" manufacturing firm. Using information about tax rates and bases for twenty states thought to compete with Missouri for new investment, the projected tax burden during the first year of operation was calculated. While the Price Waterhouse report noted that the taxes were for a "typical" manufacturing firm rather than any specific industry or firm, Missouri clearly should hope that the caution is disregarded by those firms who read the report, as Missouri appears with the second lowest tax total. Among the twenty-one states compared in the study, there was considerable variation in average tax burden.

However, without knowing the relative importance of state and local taxes on business, it is difficult to interpret the results. The State of Ohio attempted to put interstate tax comparisons on a somewhat different basis by calculating state and local business taxes per $1,000 dollars of business profit. To facilitate comparisons, a recent study (Cornia, Testa, and Stocker, 1978) for the same year, estimated wages per $1,000 of business profit. These results appear in Table 12 below.

These figures must be interpreted quite cautiously. The study assumed that profits were distributed among the states in direct proportion to nonagricultural private employment. Then total wages and total state and local business taxes in each state were used to arrive at the ratio of taxes and wages to profits. This procedure was necessary because no figures exist on actual business profits at the state level due to the fundamental ambiguity resulting from multistate firms.

There appears to be substantial variation among states in terms of the tax burden as a share of profits. The relative weight of wages is clearly much larger than that of business taxes. When calculated on an

Table 11

State of Missouri Comparative Summary Business Tax Liabilities

State	1978 First Year Total	% Higher Than Lowest State
Michigan	$389,094	—
Missouri	436,072	12.07%
Arkansas	456,660	17.36
Oklahoma	487,416	25.27
Kentucky	496,838	27.69
Iowa	526,318	35.27
Texas	555,145	42.68
Tennessee	555,784	42.84
Nebraska	574,936	47.76
New Jersey	576,158	48.08
Massachusetts	590,952	51.88
Ohio	592,811	52.36
Indiana	615,333	58.15
Minnesota	618,621	58.99
California	625,882	60.86
Kansas	659,352	69.46
New York	660,604	69.78
Wisconsin	672,309	72.79
Illinois	681,406	75.13
Connecticut	717,351	84.36
Pennsylvania	790,471	103.16

SOURCE: Summary table from *State Tax Comparison Study,* Price, Waterhouse and Co., 1978.

unweighted basis, business taxes averaged $21.6 per $100 profit, while wages averaged $379.3 per $100 profit. Clearly, equal percentage differences in average wages would be viewed with far more importance in the location decision than equal percentage differences in state and local business taxes by a business seeking to minimize would be costs. The standard deviation (again unweighted) of business taxes is $5.6, while the standard deviation for wages is $48.0. Thus, the variation among states in terms of wages is about 8.6 times greater than for taxes. This means that small differences in wage costs will usually be of much more importance to businesses than small differences in tax

Table 12

State and Local Taxes on Business Per $100 Profit and Wages Per $100 Profit: 1974

State	Taxes	Wages	State	Taxes	Wages
Maine	$21	$317	North Dakota	17	304
New Hampshire	15	324	South Carolina	18	317
Vermont	20	339	Georgia	16	326
Massachusetts	23	382	Florida	19	342
Rhode Island	23	324	Kentucky	14	366
Connecticut	27	397	Tennessee	15	323
New York	33	385	Alabama	15	350
New Jersey	25	396	Mississippi	20	284
Pennsylvania	23	386	Arkansas	14	299
Ohio	21	481	Louisiana	38	442
Indiana	18	457	Oklahoma	20	343
Illinois	23	445	Texas	23	357
Michigan	31	557	Montana	28	405
Wisconsin	24	440	Idaho	20	344
Minnesota	28	431	Wyoming	32	N/A
Iowa	14	400	Colorado	21	405
Missouri	16	382	New Mexico	27	308
North Dakota	19	323	Arizona	24	394
South Dakota	16	336	Utah	22	405
Nebraska	12	347	Nevada	22	464
Kansas	19	353	Washington	26	416
Delaware	23	461	Oregon	19	385
Maryland	21	336	California	32	409
Virginia	18	334	Alaska	19	490
West Virginia	26	400	Hawaii	20	375

SOURCE: "State and Local Fiscal Incentives and Economic Development," Cornia, G., Testa, A., and Stocker, F., Urban and Regional Development Series No. 4, Academy for Contemporary Problems, Columbus, Ohio, 1978.

burdens (this may indicate that the competition among states on the basis of taxes is more fierce than competition in labor markets). If tax incentives are viewed as a means to offset wage differences, they would typically have to be very large—much larger than those currently in use.

Williams (1967), in a more detailed study of relative costs of doing business in a number of states, constructed average costs structures, including a measure of state and local tax burden, for manufacturing industries in the upper Midwest. The study was conducted with a focus on Minnesota, and used industries at the level of detail described by the two- and four-digit industries of the Standard Industrial Classification (for example, primary metals is a two digit industry, while gray iron foundries, within primary metals, is a four digit industry). For each industry, states were ranked in terms of total average cost with and without state and local business taxes. With taxes included it was found that taxes ranged from 1.82 percent down to .26 percent of the value of shipments (or sales). In the industry with the greatest tax advantage for Minnesota, taxes as a percentage of the value of shipments were only one-fourth the level of the highest state in the ranking. In the area of greatest tax disadvantage, the Minnesota tax burden was nearly five times as high as the state with lowest tax ranking.

Such figures must be viewed in the context of other cost differences. The Williams study attempted to do this by determining the effect on the overall cost ranking of eliminating all state and local taxes. Among the more aggregated two-digit industries, the rankings of states changed in only two cases, and then by only one position. Among the more detailed four-digit industries, the ranking changed only ten times out of thirty-eight industries. Thus, in the majority of industries, state and local taxes did not appear to distort the relative cost structure of competing states (even without taking into account the possibility that the tax differences reflected different preferences for state and local services).

Williams also evaluated the effect on Minnesota's ranking of eliminating the Minnesota business taxes while retaining those of other states. In some ways, this is similar to the provision of tax incentives by one state without a response from others. As seen in Table 13, Minnesota would change total cost ranking in two of the two-digit industries, and in twenty of the thirty eight four-digit industries. However, it is quite unlikely that Minnesota would be able to drop business taxes without a competitive response, without dropping valuable business services, or without significantly increasing personal taxes to the point that it influenced wage costs.

In an interesting exercise, Williams calculated the magnitude of the
tax reduction required for Minnesota to improve its competitive

Table 13

The Effect of Tax Reduction on Minnesota's Relative Cost Position

Industry	Net Change in Ranking if only Minnesota's Taxes Eliminated	% Tax Reduction Needed to Improve Rank One Position	Industry	Net Change in Ranking if only Minnesota's Taxes Eliminated	% Tax Reduction Needed to Improve Rank One Position
Two-Digit Industries					
Lumber and wood products	0	—	Motors and generators	1	69
Stone, clay, and glass	0	—	Fabricated plate shops	3	39
Machinery, except electrical	0	—	Trucks and tractors	0	243
Pulp and paper	0	299	Sporting goods	1	33
Petroleum and coal	0	564	Knit outerwear	1	30
Fabricated metal products	0	156	Fabricated structural steel	1	14
Transportation equipment	0	136	Concrete brick and block	0	129
Printing and publishing	5	21	Games and toys	0	155
Rubber products	0	214	Candy	0	155
Chemicals	1	70	Machine tools	0	130
Primary metals	0	133	Bolts, nuts, etc.	1	32
Food and kindred products	0	136	Truck and bus bodies	3	14
			Drugs	0	321
Four-Digit Industries			Nonferrous foundries	1	72
			Grain mill products	1	35
Malt Liquors	0	—	Book printing	0	337
House furnishings	0	—	Mattresses and springs	2	53
Screw machine products	0	—	Food products machinery	1	95
Millwork plants	0	1,285	Meat packing	8	34
Wood preserving	1	46	Prepared animal feed	1	39
Printing Machinery	0	195	Wood furniture	5	2
Boat building	0	112	Upholstered furniture	0	618
Grease and tallow	0	333	Lithography	1	22
Underwear	0	1,253	Sheet metal work	4	10
Prefabricated wood buildings	2	62	Bakery products	3	11
Shoes	0	842	Commercial printing	2	45
Gray iron foundries	0	167			

SOURCE: Tables 2 and 3, "A Measure of the Impact of State and Local Taxes on Industry Location," Williams, W., Journal of Regional Science, Vol. 7, Summer 1967, no. 1.

position with regard to at least one other state (allowing for reductions of greater than 100% or a net subsidy). As shown in Table 13, in many cases large multiples of present taxes would be required in tax reductions or refundable tax credits to offset nontax interstate differentials.

STATISTICAL APPROACHES TO MEASURING THE INFLUENCES OF TAXES[1]

There exists a variety of statistical approaches available to examine the relationship between state and local taxes on business and investment and employment. The goal of using statistical approaches is to force a researcher to specify more precisely what he expects to find, and to seek empirical evidence to confirm or deny the expectation. There is a danger that simple statistical approaches will neglect the complexities inherent in business investment decisions, and find misleading results. The most appropriate method of statistical investigation in this area is to correctly specify an equation with investment or employment by state and industry as the dependent variable—with independent variables representing as many of the factors thought to influence the business decisions as can be quantified—and estimate the coefficient of the variable representing state business tax burden. If the equation is properly specified, and the tax variable accurately captures differences among states, the elasticity or investment or employment with respect to taxes can be derived. However, as discussed previously, there are significant difficulties in properly specifying the equation, capturing offsetting benefits of taxation, and measuring the tax burden. With very few exceptions, empirical work in industrial location has been carried out without explicit discussion of these problems.

The earliest statistical attempt to relate taxation to state development appeared in *An Econometric Model of Postwar State Industrial Development* (Thompson and Mattila, 1959). In part, this study is important because it is frequently cited as a basis for asserting that state taxes do not significantly influence state industrial development. The study attempted to explain differences among states in manufacturing employment growth over the period 1947-1954. The methodology employed incorporated both simple correlations and ordinary least squares regression equations. Their dependent variables were both absolute and percentage employment growth in manufacturing industries at the two-digit level of sectoral detail. As independent variables, they tested changes in state population, changes in state personal income, average manufacturing wages, percent of the work force in unions, average educational levels, overall manufacturing investment by state, industry investment by state in 1947, and industry employment in 1947. To test the importance of state tax burdens, they used two alternative variables: state and local taxes as a percent of state personal income in 1953, and an estimate of state and local taxes paid per nonagricultural business employee in 1953. Neither measure attempts to separate out taxes with an initial impact on business. A major conceptual problem arises in attempting to explain growth over a period beginning in 1947 with tax burden measures for 1953. Unless relative taxes did not change among states over the time period, this method must assume that businesses could accurately forecast future taxes, since businesses making investment and employment decisions in 1947, 1948, 1949, 1950, 1951, and 1952 did not have access to 1953 tax information.

Thompson and Mattila first examined simple correlations between each of their employment variables and each independent variable. In the case of the tax burden variables, the only significant negative correlation was found for the apparel industry and taxes per employee. The importance of this finding is minimized by realizing that both New York and New England, relatively high tax areas, were losing a significant portion of their apparel industry in this same time period. The relative importance of taxes, of course, cannot be separated using simple correlation methods.

Thompson and Mattila also estimated regression equations with ordinary least squares. Again, the only industry with a significant and negative coefficient between employment growth and tax burden was the apparel industry (although their t-statistic in this case was only 1.74). These overall regression results have been widely cited as demonstrating the insignificance of state and local taxes in influencing the relative rates of state development and interstate industrial location choices.

Campbell (1965) employed similar correlation methods to come to similar conclusions. In this study, simple correlations were calculated between development indicators such as income per capita, production per capita, and percent employment growth, and tax measures such as per capita state and local expenditures and per capita taxes. Unfortunately, the tax measures employed 1962 information to be correlated with 1959 development indicators, implicitly assuming excellent forecasting ability among the business community. In all cases, Campbell found positive and significant correlation coefficients, and concluded that taxes measured in per capita terms move with economic activity. The study concluded that the frequently assumed negative relationship between high taxes and economic activity does not exist. This is a somewhat strong conclusion given the methodological problems in the study.

Sacks (1965) sought to relate a more narrow version of tax burden to development with similar methodologies. This study defined a set of state and local taxes as business taxes, and developed measures of business taxes per capita, business property taxes per capita, and business taxes as a percent of total taxes. As development indicators, he used per capita income received and per capita production. In all cases, Sacks found significant and positive correlation coefficients between tax measures and development indicators. The study concluded that no evidence exists to indicate that high business taxes or a high business share of total taxes are a deterrent to economic development.

Struyk (1967) examines two hypotheses: (1) that regions with low taxes will grow more rapidly than other regions with high taxes, and (2) that regions with higher public services will grow more rapidly than regions with lower public services. He uses the growth of fifty cities in twenty four states as the units of observation. For the period 1950-1960, the study attempted to explain the growth of population and per capita income in terms of the levels and percentage change in per capita state taxes and per capita local taxes. Struyk found a significant and negative coefficient for the total state and total local taxes growth rate variable in explaining changes in population growth (because the study did not report actual coefficients or equations, it is not possible to be more specific). The tax variables had insignificant and inconsistent coefficients when used to explain changes in income. In *separate* regressions, Struyk attempted to relate public expenditures as a measure of service levels (no differentiation by type of service) and growth. No consistent results were found. Thus, Struyk reported that tax differentials influenced population growth but not income growth, and that expenditure levels had no observable effect on growth.

Carlton (1979) attempted to determine the relative importance of a number of factors in the location choices of new companies and new branch plants in the plastic products, electronic transmitting equipment, and electronic components industries. Instead of using investment or employment as the dependent variable, Carlton used the event of a new company or new plant as the unit of observation. The time period used was 1967-1975, and the geographical unit of observation was an SMSA. The number of urban areas in the sample ranged from twenty-eight for electronic transmitting equipment to forty-two for plastic products.

For births of new firms, Carlton estimated coefficients with a conditional logit equation to predict the probability of births in each urban area. Independent variables included were wage rates, electricity costs, natural gas costs, person-hours of activity in the local industry at the beginning of the period (as a measure of "potential" entrepreneurs and agglomeration economies), the number of engineers (with a similar motivation as existing activity), unemployment rates (as a proxy for local demand), and four tax variables. The local property tax rate, the state personal income tax rate, the state corporate income tax rate, and an index reflecting the number of incentives (both fiscal and financial) were tested.

Carlton found that the birth rate in all three industries was very responsive to local wage rates. Electricity and natural gas costs were also significant and negative. Existing activity and the number of engineers—intended to measure agglomeration economies and the availability of entrepreneurs—were both significant and positive in sign.

In no case was the coefficient for either personal income tax rate or corporate income tax rate negative and significant. In two cases, the corporate income tax rate was *positive* and significant. Similarly, the coefficients on local property tax rates were not significant for any of the industries. The coefficients for the incentive index were generally *negative* but usually insignificant.

A similar approach was taken for new branch plants. In this case, all coefficients for each tax measure were insignificant. Wages were relatively less important and energy costs relatively more important than for new companies. The level of existing activity exerted a positive and significant influence on new branch plants, indicating that agglomeration economies existed.

Hodge (1978) examined the investment patterns of the apparel, furniture, and the electronics industry in forty-two cities over the period 1963 to 1975. Using pooled time series and cross-section data, Hodge's work is unique in that it includes a variable intended to capture the proximity of a city to the sources of demand for the industry. (The index was constructed using private data on sales patterns in major urban areas and the distance from each city to those urban areas.) Hodge's equation also included as dependent variables a wage cost variable, a rent index, the national growth rate of the industry, a building cost index, the national cost of capital, a supply index constructed in a manner similar to the spatial demand index, and three variables to capture tax and incentive patterns. He included the local property tax rate, the state corporate income tax rate, and an index of incentives (similar to that constructed by Carlton).

Hodge's results varied substantially among the industries. For the furniture industry, he estimated a significant and negative coefficient for both the local property tax and the state corporate income tax rate. He estimated the elasticity of investment with respect to local property tax rates at –0.35 and the elasticity with respect to state corporate income tax rates at –0.29. For the apparel industry, he found a significant and negative coefficient for the local property tax, implying an elasticity of –0.54 (although this may partially reflect the heavy weight of New York City, with a great loss of apparel and high property tax rates over his study period). The coefficient for the state corporate income tax rate was insignificant. For the electronics industry, the tax variables were all insignificant. For all industries, the coefficient on the incentive index was insignificant. Hodge noted that his findings may simple reflect an increase in the capital/labor ratio under the influence of property taxes rather than an effect on the location of investment.

Genetski and Chin (1978) represents one of the most flawed but politically significant attempts to relate state and local taxation to economic development. This study, an unpublished paper done in the research unit of the Harris Bank of Chicago, has been cited by the *Wall Street Journal* in editorials on regional policy.

The study attempted to find a relationship between growth in per capita personal income by state relative to national growth income, and relative growth in total state and local tax receipts as a percent of total state personal income. The study was cross-sectional, with changes measured over seven-year periods.

When relative income growth was regressed against relative tax levels, no significant relationship was found. State income growth appeared to be independent of the level of taxation by state and local authorities. When relative income growth was regressed against *changes* (from 1969-1976) in relative state and local tax burdens, their adjusted R^2 increased to .25. Finally, they regressed relative income growth versus changes in relative tax burden from an earlier period—1967-1974. In this case, their adjusted R^2 increased to .59. On the basis of this evidence, they argued (and the *Wall Street Journal* asserted) that relative income growth responded, with a three year lag, to relative changes in the state and local tax burden. Thus, a state which has high taxes, but reduces them slightly, will increase its growth relative to a state which has low taxes but increases them slightly.

The Genetski and Chin study suffers from fatal flaws, and is an excellent example of the use of simple statistics for political purposes. In their preferred regression, with lagged tax changes, most of the change in relative income must occur before the relevant workers, consumers, and businesses have the information about the tax change that is supposed to be influencing their behavior. Even ignoring this flaw, the use of relative changes in taxes to predict relative changes in income tells a story about the behavior of economic entities inconsistent with other observed behavior: the study asserts that economic decisionmakers ignore the level of their taxes and focus only on the direction of relative change. In effect, all decisionmakers must assume that the direction of change will continue and have a discount rate which approaches zero, in that history (as embodied in the present tax rate) is of no effect. A third flaw is the exclusion of a number of other possible variables, such as population migration, land costs, wages, climate, crime, energy costs, and any number of other factors of potential importance in explaining the general direction of economic development. As is well understood, the exclusion of relevant variables will cause bias in the estimated coefficients for remaining variables. Genetski and Chin excluded variables which all observers would agree have some effect, so that *by definition* their coefficient on the tax variable is biased. In which direction the bias exists is impossible to determine without further study. Finally, it is possible to tell an entirely different story than assumed by Genetski and Chin. It is quite possible that it is previous slow relative growth which causes changes in relative tax rates rather than the reverse. To test this possibility, we ran a number of alternative regressions (the detailed results are available from the author). In these regressions, the relative change in tax burden was used as the *dependent* variable, and regressed against relative change in income, with income changes lagged three years. In a number of time periods, this reverse relationship appears to be as strong as the one described by Genetski and Chin. Undoubtedly both factors are at work. However, given the conceptual and methodological errors of the underlying study, it is not possible to infer *any* conclusions about the true relationships between state and local taxes and economic development. To assert, as the *Wall Street Journal* does, that research now shows that relative changes in tax burden will lead to increased development is completely without justification and can be understood only as a rhetorical statement.

Summary of Statistical Investigations

Only limited conclusions can be drawn from previous statistical research in this area. Few studies have focused directly on investment or employment. Most other studies, such as those of Campbell, Sacks, Genetski and Chin, and Struyk, are fundamentally flawed in methodology, either through sole reliance on simple correlation or by excluding variables known to be important. Thompson and Mattila, Carlton, and Hodge approach the issue more directly and with fewer methodological flaws. None sufficiently address the difficult issue of developing an appropriate measure of state and local taxes on business. Of these studies, only Hodge found a significant and negative effect of state corporate income taxes on the investment of any sector (in his case furniture). Only Hodge and Carlton attempted to explicitly measure the influence of incentives (through the construction of an incentive index) on investment, and they detected no significant effects. However, it is not possible to place a great deal of confidence in these results, since there is no information on the relative size or targeting of the incentives. Only if businesses took an extremely naive view of incentives, and considered them without determining their relative size or eligibility, would such an aggregate index be an acceptable measure.

EVIDENCE FROM SURVEYS AND INTERVIEWS

In terms of simple number, the largest body of evidence relating tax structure to economic development comes from surveys and interviews with businesses. There is substantial controversy over the value of evidence gained in this manner because of a number of weaknesses with the methods usually used.

The typical survey instrument and methodology consists of drawing up a long list of factors which the researcher believes may influence industrial location. The survey is sent to a firm, which in some cases has recently located in a limited geographical area, and in other cases has no particular geographical orientation. The firm is asked to rank the factors in terms of importance, or state whether or not they had any influence, or place the factors into such categories as critical, significant, modest importance, and no importance. The results are used by public development agencies or private advocacy groups to recommend (or rationalize) changes in development policy. Some factor such as taxes or tax incentives is usually included so that local development officials can determine whether or not taxes or lack of incentives are deterring investment.

At least six substantial criticisms have been levied against survey methods. First, the questions asked tend to make a substantial difference in the answers obtained. In particular, different answers are obtained if, "What factors should be considered in a location decision?" is asked rather than "what factors were considered in your location decision?" Second, if questions are asked about a past location decision in a given geographical area, the sample is restricted to those firms which found the area acceptable, rather than to those firms which considered the area. Third, there is usually no information contained in the survey to indicate the position of the respondent, and it probably makes a difference whether it was the director of labor relations, the real estate manager, the corporate treasurer, or the president of the company. Fourth, the specific factors included in the survey usually contain at least some ambiguity in their interpretation (to be stated precisely would lengthen the survey instrument beyond what most respondents would consider filling out). Fifth, it can be presumed that there is an incentive for strategic behavior on the part of respondents when questions of public policy such as tax policy are asked. If a respondent believes legislators or elected officials will be influenced by the survey, there is an incentive to answer by exaggerating the importance of taxes. Sixth, few surveys include questions about the process of geographical selection, or differentiate between selction of a region versus selection of a specific site. While both logic and industrial location analysts indicate that larger firms search for new locations in a multistate process, almost no surveys attempt to separate out these stages in their questions. Finally, it is difficult to interpret the results of most surveys in an anlytical manner. Learning that a certain portion of respondents considered taxes "of moderate importance" in choosing a location gives relatively little information about the magnitude of the response to changes in tax levels or incentives.

The best review of surveys undertaken prior to 1964 is provided in Morgan (1964). This study reviewed twenty-four survey and interview studies of firms in all areas of the nation. Morgan found general consensus among the survey results. Even though there was considerable variation in the specific questions asked, the types of firms in the sample, and the areas of the country, taxes and financial inducements were consistently ranked in the bottom one-fifth or one-tenth of factors mentioned by respondents. In Morgan's review, surveys were examined from the point of view of whether the results indicated that taxes or financial inducements were ranked of primary significance, some significance, or little significance by the average respondent. As shown in Table 14 below, in the thirteen surveys which specifically included incentives, such inducements were, on average, always of little or no importance. Overall business taxes, as distinct from incentives, were included in all seventeen surveys. They were considered of primary importance (along with wages, markets, and availability of raw materials) in one survey, of some significance in three surveys, and of little significance in the remaining thirteen surveys.

Table 14

Relative Importance of Location Factors in 17 Surveys

	Number of surveys in which a factor was described as of:		
Factor	Primary Significance	Some Significance	Little Significance
Markets	16	1	0
Labor	10	7	0
Raw Materials	10	6	0
Transportation	7	10	0
Taxes	1	3	13
Financial Incentives	0	0	13

SOURCE: Table 2, "The Effects of State and Local Tax and Financial Inducements on Industrial Location," Morgan, W. unpublished Ph.D. dissertation, University of Colorado, 1964.

Further insight can be gained by examining some of the actual numbers underlying Morgan's review. Even in cases where the overall rating in a survey is that taxes are of minor importance, some firms may have been substantially influenced by interstate tax differences (although it should be noted that most of the surveys reviewed by Morgan did not attempt to determine the stage of the location decision at which various factors became important). In a study of 253 businesses which had located in Colorado between 1948 and 1957, 12.7 percent indicated that they had given some consideration to state and local taxes. In a survey of 752 firms locating in Florida in 1956 and 1957, only one firm mentioned state and local taxes as the primary factor influencing its location choice. When 102 Georgia firms were asked what Georgia should do, in 1956, to attract more firms, only three firms mentioned tax concessions. In a survey of 118 firms which located in Maryland between 1946 and 1951, only four firms considered state and local taxes to be significant in their decision. In a survey of 241 (primarily new) New Jersey firms in 1958, 34 percent stated that business taxes were very important in their location decisions (this was the survey in which taxes were determined to be of primary significance). Of 166 firms locating in Oregon between 1948 and 1953, 3 percent mentioned that state and local taxes strongly influenced their choice. In a national survey by *Business Week* in which 283 firms were asked which factors *should* be considered in a location decision (not which were considered for a specific decision), 14 percent considered state and local taxes to be of some importance. In a study of 350 Texas firms in 1953-1954, five firms ranked state and local taxes among the five most important factors in their choice. These figures should not be taken as estimates of the proportion of firms which would not have located in some area if taxes were higher or incentives not offered. These proportions are at best an upper bound on the estimates for that question.

Morgan also reviewed seven studies based on personal interviews with corporate decisionmakers. Such interviews share many of the shortcomings of mail surveys, but typically have the advantages of clearly identifying the appropriate decision-maker and not restricting possible answers to those preselected by the researcher. However, as in the surveys, there was general agreement among the interview studies. As seen in Table 15 below, markets were considered to be the most important factor, followed by labor, raw materials, and transportation. In not one of the interview studies reviewed by Morgan were either taxes or financial incentives considered of primary or secondary importance.

In an early study not reviewed in Morgan (1964), Mueller and Morgan (1962, unrelated), used personal interviews to determine the factors underlying the locational choices of manufacturing firms in

Table 15

Relative Importance of Location Factors in 7 Interview Studies

Factor	Number of studies in which a factor was described as of:		
	Primary Significance	Some Significance	Little Significance
Markets	6	1	0
Labor	3	4	0
Raw Materials	3	4	0
Transportation	0	6	1
Taxes	0	0	7
Financial Incentives	0	0	7

SOURCE: Table 4, "The Effects of State and Local Tax and Financial Inducements on Industrial Location," Morgan, W. unpublished Ph.D. dissertation, University of Colorado, 1964.

Michigan. The study differentiated between factors which the firms felt *should* be important in locating a plant and factors which had been important in locating the specific plant of the corporate decisionmaker. In ranking factors, executives were asked to name the five factors which should be of most importance. Six factors were named by firms representing at least 50 percent of employment in the sample. In order of mention, they were labor costs, proximity to markets, availability of skilled labor, industrial climate, the tax bill, and proximity to raw materials. The tax bill was mentioned among the five most important factors in firms representing 52 percent of sample employment.

Mueller and Morgan obtained very different results when executives were asked to report the factors that influenced their specific plant to be located in Michigan (as opposed to the choice of a particular site within Michigan). With this question, nontraditional factors become far more important. Personal reasons were a main reason for firms with 50 percent of the employment to locate in Michigan, with the relative importance of personal reasons declining with firm size. A better tax situation was mentioned by firms representing only 1 percent of sample employment, primarily among the larger firms. Local incentives were mentioned by firms representing only 2 percent of sample employment, again concentrated among larger firms.

Stafford (1974) conducted in-depth personal interviews with a small number of manufacturing firms which had recently located in Ohio. No initial list of factors was used, with only the statements of the manufacturers indicating the relative importance of location factors. Of fourteen factors mentioned in the interviews, taxes were mentioned least frequently, and were seen as unimportant in choosing either a region or a specific site.

Inc. magazine (1980) conducted a survey of its readers to determine the factors influencing their future location choices. Firms were asked to select the three most important considerations in selecting a future site (note no distinction was made between stages of the location selection process). Various labor market factors were mentioned in the top three by 65.1 percent of the respondents, with the availability of skilled labor most important. Market location was mentioned by 56.1 percent of the respondents, with access to established markets viewed as more important than access to new markets. Transportation facilities were seen as important by 58 percent of the respondents, with highways by far the most favored. After these three factors, taxes were mentioned most frequently, ranked in the top three by 32.5 percent of the respondents. Nearly 22 percent mentioned a low tax rate in the three most important locational factors. Given the wording of the question, it is not possible to determine how frequently taxes were thought to be the critical location factor. Since the questions were asked concerning a hypothetical location rather than a specific past decision, it is possible that these traditional market and cost factors were mentioned more frequently than they will actually apply.

Somewhat surprisingly, only two studies have actually asked firms known to have received tax incentives about the relative weight of the incentive in their location decision. Ross (1953) surveyed firms in Louisiana which had asked for and received state property tax exemptions. Dorgan (1980) surveyed firms in North Dakota which received exemption from local property taxation.

Among other questions, the Ross study asked firms directly whether they would have developed their project without the tax exemption, and whether or not they would have located their plant in Louisiana without the exemption. In the absence of the exemption, 15.8 percent of the firms stated that they would not have developed their new plant or expansion. Also, 17 percent stated that they would not have developed their plant in Louisiana without the exemption. Ross also asked about the deciding factor in both the investment decision and the location decision, and discovered significant inconsistencies in the replies. Thus, while only 5.4 percent of all respondents indicated that the tax exemption was the deciding factor in undertaking their investment, 15.8 percent, when asked in a separate portion of the survey, indicated that they would not have undertaken the investment without the subsidy. Similarly, while only 3.1 percent stated that the exemption was the deciding factor in locating their investment in Louisiana, 17 percent indicated that they would not have located in

Louisiana without the subsidy. These discrepancies are probably a good measure of the willingness of firms to overestimate the influence of incentives in answering the questions. Ross concluded that approximately 7 percent of the dollar value of the investments would have been lost to the state if the subsidy program was not in effect. The remainder received windfall benefits from the tax reductions.

Dorgan did not include such specific questions, and only asked firms for the "major" factors in their location decision. As seen in Table 16, ten of the 125 firms responding to the survey indicated that the tax incentive was a major factor in their location decision. However, for some of the ten firms, a "major" influence need not have been the deciding or marginal influence. Thus the results should be interpreted as saying that no more than ten out of the sample would not have located in North Dakota, with the real number somewhat less (a more precisely worded question would have been valuable). However, there were significant differences in effect among types of firms, with 75 percent of the large agricultural products processing cooperatives reporting a major factor, 15.4 percent of the out-of-state headquarters firms reporting a major factor, and only 3.2 percent of the North Dakota-based firms indicating a major effect.

Table 16

Response of Firms to North Dakota Property Tax Incentives

	Number of Firms Receiving Incentives	Number of Firms Where Incentive Was a Major Factor in Location
Firms based out of state	26	4 (15.4%)
North Dakota firms	95	3 (3.2%)
Large regional cooperatives	4	3 (75.0%)

SOURCE: Table A, "North Dakota's New Industry Tax Exemption: Economic Incentive or Tax Giveaway?", Bryon Dorgan, North Dakota State Tax Commissioner, January 1980.

Summary of Evidence from Surveys and Interviews
Taking into account the wide diversity of techniques, types of respondent companies, and geographical areas, the consistency of findings from surveys and interviews is striking. Even disregarding the existence of reasons to overestimate the importance of business taxes and incentives, businesses themselves agree that the fiscal considerations and incentives are of relatively little importance in their location decision. It is quite rare for more than 10 percent of respondents to indicate that taxes were of any significance in a location decision, with the majority of studies showing significantly

less that 10 percent. Unfortunately, most of the studies ask the wrong questions if the intent is to determine the marginal effect of incentives and changes in tax structures. Thus, even the 10 percent finding should be considered an upper bound.

EVIDENCE FROM STUDIES ATTEMPTING TO MEASURE THE PUBLIC RETURN Only two studies have attempted to determine the public rate of return or ratio of benefits to costs for industrial location subsidies. Conceptually, such studies should follow the public investment framework discussed in Chapter Three, in identifying those investments which were affected and the accompanying flow of income which should be counted at the relevant state or local level. No study has attempted to analyze incentives from the national perspective.

The most detailed study was performed by Rinehart (1962) in a series of case studies of industrial firms subsidized by small towns in the rural South during the late 1950s. Rinehart attempted to estimate the direct payroll resulting from a new factory, and included indirect and induced income effects. He subtracted out the wages lost when workers left other jobs which then went unfilled. Unemployed workers were assumed to have placed no value on leisure. The costs included were tax abatements, cash grants, the value of physical improvements, and a variety of other informal inducements provided to the firm. No attempt was made to determine whether unused capacity existed in local public services (such as schools) or whether new capacity (and hence new costs) were required. After discounting both incremental income and costs at an assumed social opportunity cost of 6 percent, Rinehart converted this net present value to a level stream of perpetual income, and calculated the rate of return. Rinehart *assumed* that no investment would have occurred without the subsidies, and evaluated the rate of return from the perspective of the local community—not the state or the nation. Thus the rates of return calculated are far higher than broader analyses. The analysis was done under three different assumptions:

1. the firm produces the same income stream perpetually (no failure);
2. the firm leaves the community at the end of the study period (thus not collecting the portion of subsidy not yet granted, such as the remaining tax abatements); and
3. the firm leaves the community at the end of the study period, and the community loses the full amount of the subsidy (intended to be a worse case).

Under the assumptions, Rinehart discovered extraordinarily high rates of return (see Table 17 below). With the most optimistic assumption, the rate of return on individual subsidies ranged from 87 percent per year to 8,195 percent per year. When weighted by the amount of public subsidy, the average annual return was 492.8 percent. Under Rinehart's second assumption, the weighted average annual return dropped to 263.2 percent. It was not possible to calculate the weighted return for Rinehart's third assumption, but if the same ratio held between the unweighted and weighted as in the other case, it would be around 40 percent annually.

Table 17

Estimated Annual Rate of Return on Local Subsidies to Industry

Firm	Case 1	Case 2	Case 3
A	246%	153%	74%
B	311	178	55
C	559	169	26
D	1,506	992	375
E	181	99	28
F	87	70	18
G	220	191	32
H	1,030	665	162
I	665	380	99
J	483	459	88
K	959	810	113
L	139	154	14
M	334	221	17
N	1,373	1,000	25
O	1,116	739	216
P	515	450	52
Q	8,195	3,595	362
R	473	N/A	71
S	340	N/A	21
T	432	N/A	15
U	5,293	N/A	727
V	673	N/A	24
Unweighted Average Return	1,221.0%	613.0%	94.7%
Weighted Average Return	492.8%	263.2%	40.0%

SOURCE: Derived from information on each firm from "Rates of Return on Municipal Subsidies to Industries," Rinehart, J.R. unpublished Ph.d. dissertation, University of Virginia, 1962.

A first reaction to these returns would be that some mistake was made in arithmetic. However, upon reflection, it is clear that they provide insight into the powerful forces inducing local (not state) governments to provide incentives. For the most part, the reasons the returns are high are that it is assumed that all of the incremental income can be assigned to the public subsidy, and the fact that in many cases the subsidy was quite small, perhaps involving a small undeveloped parcel of land or a break on sewer costs. The rate of return on a one dollar public subsidy would indeed by quite high if it induced a large plant to locate in a rural Southern town. Since most officials will assume that their subsidy was the deciding factor, the local return appears extremely high. Of course, the literature reviewed above clearly indicates that these assumptions are not justified.

It is possible to adjust Rinehart's figures to take into account the possibility that some of the firms did not locate in the town because of the inducement. The critical policy question is what percentage needs to be influenced for the public subsidies to be a good investment for the community. Rinehart assumed the social opportunity cost at the time to be 6 percent. As shown in Table 18 below, it is possible to calculate the break-even probability for each firm by determining the percent of benefits used by Rinehart necessary to result in a 6 percent rate of return (although the existence of true uncertainty should dictate a significantly higher discount rate, which would necessitate a correspondingly higher breakeven rate). For the optimistic case one, the probability on average needs only to be 1.22 percent. Under the more conservative assumptions of case two, the break-even probability is still only 2.28 percent. That is, if the community believed that at least 2.28 percent of the benefits were actually induced by the subsidies, it should consider the subsidies minimally acceptable public investments.

Morgan and Hackbart (1974) used a similar conceptual framework to determine the conditions under which state-allowed local property tax abatements were acceptable public investments. They obtained estimates of the tax-exempt industrial investment made in seven states from the state development agencies for the period 1958 to 1961. They estimated the cost of the subsidies by using an average state assessment ratio and average state property tax rate, since they did not have information on the locations of the investment by individual towns. On the income side, they developed an estimate of an incremental capital/output ratio and of a state income multiplier to assess the increase in income derived from the exempted investment. They then used a variety of assumptions about the proportion of the income which was incremental (this was to account for wage losses in the jobs left by new employees as well as immigration by out-of-state residents).
They then calculated the expected benefit-cost ratio for different

Table 18

Break-even Percentage of Investment Induced by Subsidies

Firm	Case 1	Case 2	Case 3
A	2.48%	3.92%	8.11%
B	1.93	3.37	10.91
C	1.08	3.55	23.08
D	.40	.61	1.60
E	3.31	6.06	21.43
F	6.90	8.57	33.33
G	2.73	3.14	18.75
H	.58	.90	3.70
I	.90	1.58	6.06
J	1.24	1.31	6.82
K	.63	.74	5.31
L	4.32	1.11	42.86
M	1.80	2.72	35.29
N	.44	.61	24.00
O	.54	.81	2.78
P	1.17	1.33	11.54
Q	.07	.17	1.66
R	1.27		8.45
S	1.77		30.00
T	1.39		40.00
U	.11		.83
V	.89		25.00
Weighted Break-even Percentage	1.22%	2.28%	16.47%

SOURCE: Derived from Table 17.

probabilities corresponding to the chance that a given investment was actually induced by a subsidy. They did not attempt to determine the actual influence of the subsidies. Their results appear in Table 19 below.

The results of Morgan and Hackbart are generally consistent with our manipulation of Rinehart's findings. If only 1 percent of the investment is actually induced, no set of assumptions can render the subsidies a good public investment. However, if the percent induced rises to 5 percent, and both direct and indirect benefits are counted, only 25 percent of the extra income needs to be incremental to render the benefit cost ratio above one. The basic result is that only a small percentage of subsidized investment needs to be actually induced for the subsidy to be an acceptable public investment.

Table 19

Comparison of Benefits and Costs of Tax Exemption Programs

Definition of Benefits	Induced Investment as a Percentage of Total Tax Exempt Investment		
	.01	.05	.10
Benefits = 100% of Value Added			
Direct and Indirect Benefits Discount rate of .10	.88	4.38	8.77
Direct Benefits Only Discount rate of .10	.59	2.94	5.88
Benefits = 50% Value Added			
Direct and Indirect Benefits Discount rate of .10	.44	2.19	4.39
Direct Benefits Only Discount rate of .10	.29	1.47	2.94
Benefits = 25% of Value Added			
Direct and Indirect Benefits Discount rate of .10	.22	1.10	2.10
Direct Benefits Only Discount rate of .10	.15	.74	1.47
Benefits = 10% of Value Added			
Direct and Indirect Benefits Discount rate of .10	.09	.44	.88
Direct Benefits Only Discount rate of .10	.06	.29	.59

SOURCE: Table 1, "An Analysis of State and Local Industrial Tax Exemption Programs", Morgan, W. and Hackbart, M., Southern Economic Journal, October 1974.

Summary of Rate of Return Studies

A very limited amount of empirical work reviewing subsidies during the late 1950s indicates that if even a small proportion of subsidized investment is affected, the state or local subsidy is a good investment. However, the available evidence from surveys and empirical work is insufficient to determine whether or not a very small percent (perhaps 1 to 5 percent) of the total subsidized investment was actually induced. Since it is certain that all states and communities providing subsidies tremendously overestimate the importance of their subsidies, it is easy to understand why state and local governments offer an ever-increasing number of subsidies.

SUMMARY OF EMPIRICAL RESEARCH

For a field that has existed amidst public controversy for several decades, relatively little progress has been made in finally resolving the value of tax incentives for industrial investment when applied at the state level. While very difficult to measure business tax burdens between states in an appropriate manner, it is clear that many firms face interstate tax differentials that are a significant portion of their pretax income. There exists, however, near consensus from studies using surveys and interviews that tax differences or tax incentives play at best a small role in location decisions for most firms. Unfortunately nearly all of these surveys contain flaws of design.

Yet, it is also clear that from a state or local perspective, if only a relatively small share of subsidized firms are actually influenced by the tax incentive, the public investment is an acceptable one. This makes it all the more important to have empirical techniques which can identify relatively small shifts in investment or employment in response to tax differences. Unfortunately, because of the measurement problem for tax burdens, and the relatively small samples used in most econometric investigations, it is difficult to exclude the possibility of a small (but nonetheless sufficient) response.

A review of the literature must include a statement of sympathy for researchers in the field. For the most part, research must rely on unpublished data (and frequently involves the collection of primary date) and use as a key variable a state and local tax burden which is difficult to define conceptually and for which there is substantial disagreement about methodology. Nonetheless, it appears that there remains room for improvement in both survey methods and econometric investigations.

FOOTNOTES TO CHAPTER 3

[1] A significant portion of this section will rely on some familiarity with basic statistical and econometric concepts. For readers without such a background, the summary of the section should provide an adequate picture of the results of previous statistical work in the area.

4

DESCRIPTION OF
NEW EMPIRICAL RESEARCH

While there is clearly no shortage of areas in which additional information is needed, the literature review should make it clear that substantial obstacles are involved in any new eimpirical research on the effects of tax incentives. For purposes of this study, new empirical research was undertaken in four areas in which it appeared there was a reasonable prospect of obtaining useful results:

1. a rough estimation of the initial direct revenue losses to selected states as a result of automatic state tax incentives;
2. a mail survey to manufacturing firms starting or expanding in states which offer automatic income tax incentives;
3. an econometric estimation of equations designed to predict the share of new capital investment in a state for a number of two-digit manufacturing industries, using such factors as business taxes, wages, productivity, unionization, and other factors as independent variables; and
4. a benefit-cost analysis of tax incentives using the results of the mail surveys and econometric investigations.

ESTIMATION OF INITIAL REVENUE LOSSES   To place the issue of state tax incentives into some perspective, it is useful to have some estimate, however rough, of the associated initial revenue loss. This section attempts to provide an order of magnitude estimate. The tax incentives it includes are those which are provided for through a state's corporate income tax, and are available in all parts of the state. Thus, the estimates exclude all state authorized but locally administered property tax incentives (which are certain to be quite substantial), inventory and sales tax exemptions, incentives for research and development or pollution control, and all wage incentives aimed at specific classes of workers. The estimates assume that all eligible firms took advantage of the incentives, although it is likely that some of the smaller firms did not. Thus, these estimates are an upper bound on the cost of the specified incentives, but exclude many state tax incentives from any consideration.

The base for calculation of all of the revenue losses was gross investment in manufacturing in 1977 as reported in the Preliminary Census of Manufacturers for 1977. Where the incentive is available only for machinery and equipment, and not for plant and structures, it is assumed that 74.03 percent of the gross investment was in machinery and equipment, as was the case nationwide in 1976 (no comparable figures for 1977 are available).

Some states provide broad-based employment or wage incentives. In this case, the starting point remains the gross investment estimate, and it is assumed that a new job is created for each $25,000 of gross investment. This is necessarily a very crude estimate, and neglects interstate variation in capital intensity and interstate variation in the division of gross investment in terms of new investment and modernization, which have substantially different employment effects. Where the incentive is based on a percentage of new wages, it is assumed that each new employee works at an average wage equal to that prevailing among manufacturing employees in the relevant state in 1977.

While the investment figures are taken from 1977 (since no more current figures are available), all states which had legislated tax incentives as of December 1980 are included. However, in some cases the incentives legislated are not fully in place (for example, Tennessee's tax credit will not be fully implemented until 1984). Nonetheless, if passed, it is assumed that the full tax incentive was available in 1977, and applied to the 1977 investment estimate. Thus, it should be clearly understood that the estimates developed here are not estimates of the actual revenue losses incurred by states in 1977.

The estimates presented in Table 20 below are only an indication of the initial revenue loss. They do not take into account additional revenue to the state in other taxes due to possible increased activity if the incentives are effective in inducing industrial expansion. They should not be interpreted as the *net* cost to the states.

Given the assumptions, the first year revenue loss is nearly $173 million. In some states, there would be continuing losses for an additional ten years (Kansas, West Virginia). This is certainly a substantial public expenditure deserving of evaluation. Of the total revenue loss, about 92 percent is for capital subsidies and only about 8 percent is labor subsidies. Of the capital subsidies, about 87 percent is accounted for by New York and Massachusetts, due to a large share of investment and large incentives. Of the labor incentives, about 81 percent is accounted for by Louisiana and Missouri. These quite substantial sums indicate clearly that state incentives represent a large public program—one of sufficient size to merit serious evaluation.

MAIL SURVEYS   The only way to obtain information about particular business investment decisions is to survey or interview business officials directly involved in recent location choices. Personal interviews are very time consuming   *65*

Table 20

Estimates of the Initial Revenue Loss
from Selected State Tax Incentives

State	1977 Investment	Investment Incentives	Job Incentives	Total
Delaware	$ 154,000,000	$ 284,000	$ 462,000	$ 746,000
Colorado	447,400,000	223,700	894,000	1,117,700
Kansas	349,300,000	174,650	698,600	873,250
Montana	97,500,000		511,720	511,720
New York	2,715,600,000	108,624,000		108,624,000
Rhode Island	160,000,000	3,202,000		3,202,000
Massachusetts	978,300,000	29,340,000		29,340,000
New Mexico	100,800,000	2,798,334		2,798,334
North Dakota	52,900,000		242,599	242,599
West Virginia	370,100,000	3,701,000		3,701,000
Louisiana	2,167,000		8,668,000	8,668,000
Oklahoma	497,700,000	2,488,500		2,488,500
Missouri	885,800,000	664,350	2,657,400	3,321,750
Tennessee	963,200,000	7,130,570		7,130,570
		$ 158,631,104	$ 14,134,319	$ 172,765,423

SOURCE: 1977 investment figures represent estimates of gross new depreciable investment taken from the preliminary 1977 Census of Manufacturers. The tax incentives, as described in Table 9, were applied to the investment estimates as described in the text.

and limit the number of firms included in the study. Mail surveys impose difficulties in obtaining adequate response rates, but are far less expensive. For this study, the direct mail approach was taken to reach firms that had made investments in states offering automatic tax incentives. The goals of the mail survey carried out for this study were to determine answers to four general questions:

1. the extent to which firms searched for sites among more than one state;
2. the relative importance of different characteristics of competing states in influencing the choice among states;
3. the degree to which businesses were aware of state tax incentives; and
4. the effect of the tax incentive on either the location of an investment or the amount of the investment.

The survey instrument and procedures used in this study were designed to avoid many of the problems in previous surveys (the survey instruments and a detailed discussion of methodology and results are available in Appendix II.) In particular, attention was paid in the following areas:

1. New firms, new expansion investments, and new branch plants were analyzed separately. The survey instrument for expansion investments contained several additional factors not found for the other firms. These categories were used for several reasons. First, the research of Birch (1979) indicates that the majority of employment growth results from employment changes in new manufacturing firms and expansion investments, rather than new branch plants. In contrast, most state development efforts are focused on new branch plants. In addition, previous research by Oster (1979) and Schmenner (1978) indicates that there are differences in the way in which these types of firms make location choices, and in the relative weight they place on characteristics of competing states.

2. Major attempts were made to ensure that the appropriate decision-maker received the survey instrument. Unless someone directly involved in the actual decision answers the questions, it is impossible to evaluate the results. In almost all cases, the surveys were mailed to a specific person who was very likely to have been directly involved in the location decision.

3. The survey questions were specifically created assuming that location decisions were made in stages. The questions used were directed at choices among states, rather than the selection of a specific site. Firms were asked to identify important *differences* among states rather than important factors required for any state selected.

4. Survey questions were directed at specific, named investments, rather than hypothetical investments about which factors should be considered.

5. Survey questions were directed to investments made recently, so that the relevant factors were recallable. Thus, each of the new firms surveyed were started during 1979, while the new branch plants and expansions were also made during 1979.

6. Firms were asked whether or not state tax incentives existed in the state of their actual investment. They could answer yes, no, or don't know. This question appears to be unique among surveys on location choices. Only firms investing in states which actually had tax incentives during 1979 received surveys. This question allowed answers to be interpreted in light of whether or not the firms actually made a decision having known about incentives.

7. Specific questions were asked about the marginal effect of the incentive. Rather than relying on a general ranking of the influence of a tax incentive among a collection of factors, respondents were asked directly whether the tax incentive affected the location or amount of their investment.

8. The survey asked questions to differentiate the effect of a tax incentive on the location of investment from the amount of investment. It is possible that incentives simply move investment around without affecting its amount, or that investment is not moved around but is increased at the location it would have been made at in any case.

9. The survey was structured to identify strategic (that is, intentionally misleading) answers which might serve to overestimate the importance of incentives. Businesses have an incentive to overstate the importance of tax subsidies since they might believe that the surveyor would use the information to influence future tax policies.

The mail survey provided results which will be summarized in five categories (extensive detail is available in Appendix II): the degree to which firms seriously considered other states, the relative importance of state characteristics in location choices, knowledge of tax incentives, the effect of the incentives on location, and the effect of the incentives on the amount of investment. To make it easy to compare the answers among new firms, expansions, and new branch plants, they will be presented within the same section, rather than repeat the results for each category or firm.

Proportion of Firms Considering Other States

There were substantial differences among the categories of firms in their answers to the question "Did you seriously consider locating this investment in any other state?" In no category did more than half of the firms seriously consider other states as possible locations. As shown in Table 21 below, 26.7 percent of the new firms, 28.0 percent of the expansions, and 43.8 percent of the new branch plants considered other states. In general, the expansions and new branch plants were larger firms than the new companies, which may have influenced their search behavior.

Relative Importance of State Characteristics in Location Choices

Only those firms that seriously considered locating in another state were asked to indicate the relative importance of a number of factors in choosing among states. They could describe each factor as "Deciding Positive Influence," "Moderate Negative Influence," "Insignificant Influence," or "Moderate Negative Influence." They were not asked about deciding

Table 21

Percent of Respondents Considering Location in Another State

State	New Firms	Expansions	New Plants
New York	22.9%	20.0%	54.5%
Delaware	55.5	100.0	
Colorado	20.3	20.0	0
New Mexico	40.0	0	0
Montana			0
Massachusetts	34.4	30.0	33.3
Kansas	30.4	30.8	37.5
Rhode Island	33.3	25.0	50.0
Maine		0	100.0
West Virginia	33.3	66.7	100.0
North Dakota	33.3		
Total	**26.7%**	**28.0%**	**43.8%**

NOTE: Blanks represent states where no firms responded in the appropriate category.

negative influences because if they existed, they would not have located in the state. The responses, tabulated separately for new firms, expansions, and new branch plants, are shown in Tables 22, 23, and 24 below, respectively. There are clear differences in relative importance, as determined by the proportion describing each factor by level of importance, among the different types of firms.

New firms are very concerned with the size of their markets, with access to a growing market and current customers most important. Personal reasons of management are also very frequently mentioned. After these factors, a number of "supply" factors are considered to be important: access to raw materials, availability of capital, supply of skilled labor, and transportation are frequently mentioned. Familiarity with the local economy is considered quite important as well. Business taxes are of only modest importance, as are personal taxes. The political climate and air quality regulations, which are frequent topics of political discussion, are rarely considered by new businesses.

Based on the research of Schmenner (1978), a number of factors

Table 22

Relative Importance of Location Factors for New Firms Making Interstate Location Choices

	Percent of Respondents Who Consider Factor to be of:				
Factor	Deciding Positive Influence	Moderate Positive Influence	Insignificant Influence	Moderate Negative Influence	No Answer
Availability of capital	30.0%	23.3%	36.7%	4.4%	5.6%
Supply of skilled labor	24.4	31.1	36.7	3.3	4.4
Cost of skilled labor	16.7	31.1	42.2	4.4	5.6
Supply of unskilled labor	13.3	31.1	44.4	4.4	6.7
Cost of unskilled labor	15.6	24.4	47.8	6.6	5.6
Union activities	13.3	15.6	51.1	14.4	5.6
Supply of fuel and electricity	7.8	17.8	58.9	5.6	10.0
Cost of fuel and electricity	6.7	18.9	56.7	11.1	6.7
Climate	10.0	27.8	48.9	10.0	3.3
Personal reasons of management	41.1	27.8	21.1	2.2	7.8
Transportation network	24.4	34.4	32.2	5.6	3.3
Political climate	8.9	15.6	56.7	12.2	6.7
Familiarity with economy	26.7	37.8	26.7	2.2	6.7
Air quality regulation	1.1	7.8	73.3	11.1	6.7
Business tax structure	14.4	30.0	33.3	18.9	3.3
Personal tax structure	15.6	16.7	41.1	22.2	4.4
Access to raw materials	33.3	18.9	36.7	6.7	4.4
Access to present customers	52.2	23.3	20.0	1.1	3.3
Access to growing market	50.0	20.0	25.6	2.2	2.2
Land costs	17.8	16.7	47.8	11.1	6.7

SOURCES: Responses from mail survey.

peculiar to expansion investments were included in the list of factors to be evaluated by firms having made expansions in 1979. Some of these—achieving economies of scale, maintaining an intact labor force, and ease of expanding on-site—were the most frequently mentioned reasons for making investment at the present site. Market factors—both access to current customers and to a growing market— were also considered quite important. The political climate and personal reasons of management were rated quite high, as were nontraditional factors, while access to raw materials was the most important supply factor. Business taxes were the least important factor considered by those deciding on the location of expansion investments.

For new branch plants, labor market concerns—particularly the supply of both skilled and unskilled labor—were deemed most important. In addition, the presence of unions was seriously considered. In contrast to both new firms and expansions, the state business tax structure was considered generally important. Somewhat

Table 23

Relative Importance of Location Factors for Expansions Making Interstate Location Choices

Percent of Respondents Who Consider Factor to be of:

Factor	Deciding Positive Influence	Moderate Positive Influence	Insignificant Influence	Moderate Negative Influence	No Answer
Availability of capital	21.4%	28.6%	50.0%	0.0	0.0
Economies of scale realized with expansion on-site	42.9	21.4	21.4	7.1	7.1
Supply of skilled labor	21.4	50.0	28.6	0.0	0.0
Cost of skilled labor	14.3	42.9	28.6	14.3	0.0
Supply of unskilled labor	7.1	28.6	50.0	7.1	7.1
Cost of unskilled labor	7.1	35.6	42.9	14.3	0.0
Union activities	21.4	14.3	28.6	35.7	0.0
Maintain intact labor force	42.9	35.7	21.4	0.0	0.0
Supply of fuel and electricity	21.4	21.4	42.9	14.3	0.0
Cost of fuel and electricity	14.3	28.6	35.7	21.4	0.0
Climate	7.1	28.6	64.3	0.0	0.0
Personal reasons of management	28.6	21.4	42.9	7.1	0.0
Product line or production process not easily divided	14.3	42.9	35.7	7.1	0.0
Transportation network	14.3	42.9	42.9	0.0	0.0
Political climate	28.6	7.1	42.9	21.4	0.0
Familiarity with economy	7.1	14.3	78.6	0.0	0.0
Air quality regulation	0.0	14.3	71.4	14.3	0.0
Ease of expanding on-site	42.9	28.6	28.6	0.0	0.0
Business tax structure	0.0	50.0	28.6	21.4	0.0
Personal tax structure	14.3	21.4	42.9	21.4	0.0
Access to raw materials	28.6	35.7	35.7	0.0	0.0
Access to present customers	28.6	28.6	42.9	0.0	0.0
Access to growing market	21.4	21.4	57.1	0.0	0.0
Land costs	7.1	35.7	42.9	14.3	0.0

SOURCE: Reponses from mail survey.

surprisingly, market factors—either access to a growing market or to current customers—were seen as relatively unimportant.

Knowledge of State Tax Incentives State tax incentives can be an effective development tool only if business decisionmakers are aware of them. As shown in Table 25 below, most firms are not aware of incentives. Among new firms, less than a fifth of the firms were aware that incentives existed in the state of their actual location. Among expansions, 36 percent were aware of the incentives. Since such firms did not generally consider other states with any more seriousness than new firms, this higher proportion may reflect the somewhat larger size of the firms. Among

Table 24

Relative Importance of Location Factors for
New Branch Plants Making Interstate Location Choices

Percent of Respondents Who Consider Factor to be of:

Factor	Deciding Positive Influence	Moderate Positive Influence	Insignificant Influence	Moderate Negative Influence	No Answer
Availability of capital	21.4%	42.9%	35.7%	0.0%	0.0%
Supply of skilled labor	64.3	14.3	14.3	0.0	7.0
Cost of skilled labor	21.4	64.3	7.1	7.1	0.0
Supply of unskilled labor	35.7	7.1	42.9	0.0	14.0
Cost of unskilled labor	7.1	28.6	42.9	7.1	14.0
Union activities	35.7	14.3	28.6	14.3	7.0
Supply of fuel and electricity	14.3	28.6	42.9	0.0	14.0
Cost of fuel and electricity	14.3	21.4	42.9	7.1	14.0
Climate	7.1	14.3	57.1	14.3	7.0
Personal reasons of management	28.6	28.6	35.7	0.0	7.0
Transportation network	28.6	21.4	35.7	7.1	7.0
Political climate	21.4	21.4	35.7	7.1	14.0
Familiarity with economy	0.0	28.6	57.1	0.0	14.0
Air quality regulation	0.0	21.4	64.3	0.0	14.0
Business tax structure	35.7	7.1	50.0	0.0	7.0
Personal tax structure	7.1	21.4	35.7	21.4	14.0
Access to raw materials	21.4	28.6	50.0	0.0	0.0
Access to present customers	14.3	28.6	50.0	7.1	0.0
Access to growing market	14.3	7.1	57.1	7.1	14.0
Land costs	21.4	35.7	35.7	0.0	7.0

SOURCE: Responses from mail surveys.

new branch plants, half of the firms were aware of state tax incentives (90 percent of the firms in New York), which probably reflects the more intense comparison of states by those considering new branch plants. Among new firms and expansions, more firms claimed that tax incentives did not exist (they could have indicated that they did not know) than correctly stated that they did.

Effect of the Tax Incentives on Location Decisions

Those firms which correctly indicated that state tax incentives were available were asked whether they would have located in another state if no incentive had been available. A number of firms which indicated that they would have located elsewhere had previously stated that they did not seriously consider other states—a clearly strategic set of answers. After eliminating these and similar answers, 3.3 percent of the new firms, none of the expansions, and 6.3 percent of the new branch plants

Table 25

Knowledge of Tax Incentives Among
New Firms, Expansions, and New Plants by State

State	New Firms	Expansions	New Plants
New York	28.2%	70.0%	90.0%
Delaware	22.2	100.0	
Colorado	20.3	20.0	0
New Mexico	20.0	50.0	
Montana	0		0
Massachusetts	13.3	0	0
Kansas	8.7	38.5	50.0
Rhode Island	14.8	25.0	50.0
Maine	*	0	50.0
West Virginia	0	66.7	0
North Dakota	0		
Total	**19.6%**	**36.0%**	**50.0%**

*New firms were not surveyed in Maine because they are not generally eligible for the available tax incentives

NOTE: Blanks represent cases where there were no responses.

indicated that they would have located in another state in the absence of tax incentives.

Effect of the Tax Incentives on the Amount Invested In contrast to the all or none aspect of a location decision, some firms might have changed their amount of investment—but not location—in response to a tax incentive. The change in amount may reflect either a change in the capital/labor ratio or simply a scale change in the overall project. In contrast to the prior question on location of investment, it was not possible to structure the amount question to detect misleading answers, since it is perfectly possible for a firm not have considered other locations but to respond to a tax incentive by changing the amount of investment. Thus, including any possible strategic answers, 7.7 percent of the new firms, 12 percent of the expansions, and 21.9 percent of the new plants indicated that they would have reduced their investment in the absence of a tax incentive. These proportions must be considered as upper bounds, and it is likely that the real figures are somewhat lower. However, simply knowing the proportion of firms which would have reduced their investment does not indicate how much they would have reduced their investment, and a specific question asking for such estimates was not asked.

Summary of the Results of the Mail Survey   For the most part, the results of the mail survey correspond to common sense. More branch plants consider locating in another state than new firms or expansions, but for the most part, less than half of all new investments are made as a result of a multistate search for a new location. There are differences among firms in the relative importance of state characteristics for location decisions, but only among new branch plants do business taxes assume any major importance. A majority of firms are unaware of state tax incentives, with many firms incorrectly asserting that no tax incentives are available. New branch plants are most likely to be aware of incentives, perhaps because they search more widely and are most courted by state and local development organizations. Only a very small portion of firms change their location choices because of state tax incentives, but a larger proportion of businesses claim to have increased their investment (although in an unknown amount).

ECONOMETRIC INVESTIGATIONS

It is quite clear that many factors influence the location decision for most manufacturing investments. The survey method relies upon the personal interpretation of business executives to assign relative weights to each factor. An alternative method is to observe actual patterns of investments among states, and attempt to relate those patterns to interstate differences in location factors. The standard methodology used in such an exercise is to use multiple regression techniques to estimate an equation which relates the value of a "dependent" variable, such as investment, to the values of "independent" variables as they vary across states. In general, if there are enough variables (that is, if the researcher has identified most of the factors which affect the outcome) and sufficient observations (one observation is never enough), and the underlying relationships among variables are reflected in the form of the equation (that is, only the relative weights are at issue), it is possible to make reasonable estimates of the impact of changes in the value of independent variables on the dependent variable.

As noted above, the end result of a multiple regression analysis is an equation relating the dependent variable to the independent variables. For each independent variable, the statistical technique estimates a "coefficient," which describes the magnitude of the effect of changes in the independent variables on the value of the dependent variable. To understand this, consider the following example. In an equation in which the dependent variable is employment, measured in millions, average wage rates might be included as an independent variable. If the estimated coefficient was -2.0, it means that if average wages increased by one unit, say from $4.00 to $5.00, the number of jobs would decrease by two million.

Statistical significance is a concept needed to interpret the results of multiple regression analysis. It allows the researcher to determine the validity of the estimated coefficients. Typically, an estimated coefficient is considered either significant or insignificant, which is shorthand for saying whether the researcher has sufficient confidence that the true coefficient is different from zero (and thus considered insignificant). In cases where a coefficient is statistically significant, the estimated value of the coefficient is the best "guess" of the true relationship between the independent and dependent variables. In cases where the coefficient is statistically insignificant, the best assumption is that the value of the coefficient is zero, which implies that the independent variable in question has no impact on the dependent variable.

General Methodology   In the investigations reported here, the dependent variable used was a state's share of total national gross investment in a particular industry during 1977. At issue is whether the share of national investment made in a given state is systematically influenced by such factors as the business or personal tax burdens, wage levels, labor productivity, or other similar factors. The statistical techniques employed calculated coefficients for each variable, which can be used to estimate the relative importance of different location determinants. In particular, we were interested in whether or not the coefficients calculated for different measures of the business tax burden are significant, and if so, in their sign and magnitude.

Equations were estimated for thirteen manufacturing industries at the two-digit SIC level of detail: Food and Kindred Products; Textiles; Paper and Allied Products; Chemicals; Petroleum and Coal Products; Rubber and Miscellaneous Plastic Products; Stone, Clay, and Glass; Primary Metals; Fabricated Metal Products; Nonelectrical Machinery; Electrical Machinery; Transportation Equipment; and Instruments.

A number of different variables were used in each equation. Some variables had different values for each industry in every state: two measures of the business tax burden, two measures of labor productivity, the average wage rate, and the state's share of national employment. A number of variables varied among states but had the same value for each industry within the state: temperature, the growth rate of union membership, the proportion of the labor force in unions, personal tax burden, the growth rate of population, population   75 density, per capita personal income, the growth rate of personal income, energy costs, and the proportion of personal income used for welfare programs. Precise descriptions of each of the variables are available in Appendix III.

Since they are the critical variables for this study, the two measures of business tax burden require some explanation. For purposes of the econometric analyses (and discussion here), the measures were designated TAXLOAD and ORDERST. TAXLOAD generally is the actual dollar value of the state and local taxes paid by a hypothetical corporation in a given industry in various states (the concept underlying the tax burden estimates presented in Table 5). In contrast, ORDERST is a measure of the rank of a given state in an ordering of all of the states by industry tax burden. In using ORDERST, it is assumed that more confidence should be placed in the ranking of states by business tax burden than on the specific number calculated and used for TAXLOAD.

In some cases, previous research and economic theory would predict that increases in the value of a variable should increase a state's share of national investment: measures of labor productivity, population growth, per capita income, and income growth. In other cases, previous research would predict that increases in the value of a variable should lead to a decrease in investment share: wage rates, population density (as proxy for land costs), and welfare costs. For the various business and personal tax measures, it is theoretically impossible to predict the direction of influence since benefits and costs must be balanced, but anecdotal evidence indicates that it should be negative for both business and personal taxes.

A major caveat is in order before examining the results. Only one year of investment data was used for the analysis due to the major task of calculating tax burdens. Ideally, the analysis would incorporate the experience of more years, and the results of the current investigation should be interpreted with caution.

Presentation of Results   By testing a number of combinations of variables, a large number of different equations (and thus coefficients) were estimated. Because the focus of this research is on the effect of business taxes, only results for business taxes will be presented in the text (with more detailed results shown in Appendix III). These results are presented in Table 26 below, reporting the significance and elasticities of TAXLOAD and ORDERST in the best equations. Frequently, the primary difference between the equations was a simple substitution of ORDERST for TAXLOAD.

For the most part, the single most important determinant of current investment in an industry is the current location of employment. This result holds regardless of the measure used for business tax burden,

Table 26

Summary of Significance and Elasticities for Business Tax Measures*

Industry	TAXLOAD Significance	Elasticity	ORDERST Significance	Elasticity
Food: 20	insignificant		insignificant	
Textile: 22	insignificant		insignificant	
Paper: 26	insignificant		insignificant	
Chemicals: 28	insignificant		.094	−.020
Petroleum	insignificant		.067	−.013
Rubber: 30	.009	−.176	.007	−.004
Stone: 32	insignificant		insignificant	
Primary Metals: 33	insignificant		insignificant	
Fabricated Metals: 34	insignificant		.035	−.002
Machinery: 35	insignificant		insignificant	
Electronics: 36	insignificant		insignificant	
Transportation: 37	.087	+.176	.061	+.001
Instruments: 38	insignificant		insignificant	

*Where the coefficient is insignificant, no elasticity is reported because the best estimate of the coefficient is zero.

SOURCE: Derived from the tables reporting regression results for each industry in Appendix Three.

and is generally consistent with the finding of the mail survey that most firms did not seriously consider locating in other states.

There is substantially more diversity among industries in the relative importance of the business tax measures. For each industry and each measure of tax burden, two results are presented: the level of statistical significance and the estimated elasticity of the share of new investment with respect to the tax measure. In most statistical studies, a variable is considered statistically significant only below the .10 level of confidence (or frequently, the more restrictive .05 level). As seen in Table 26 below, TAXLOAD is significant at the .10 level for only two industries—Rubber (significant at the .05 level) and Transportation. However, contrary to conventional wisdom, the results indicate that increases in TAXLOAD result in increases in investment share for Transportation. In both industries, the elasticity is quite small, at negative .176 for Rubber and positive .176 for Transportation. This should be interpreted as follows: a 1 percent increase in business taxes on the Rubber industry by a given state will result in a .176 percent loss of investment share and conversely for Transportation.

However, when ORDERST is used as a measure of business tax burden, it is statistically significant in five industries: Chemicals, Petroleum, Rubber, Fabricated Metals, and Transportation. Except for Transportation, an increased business tax burden leads to a   77 decrease in investment share. However, the elasticity of investment share is very small, ranging from –.002 to –.020. While it is not possible to directly translate this into a reflection of change of taxes (because ORDERST is a measure of the rank of a state, not the actual taxes), this in general is a very low elasticity.

The econometric results should not be taken as definitive, given the very serious problems with using only one year for an investment study. However, it is reasonable to interpret them as providing additional support for the hypothesis that for most firms, interstate differences in business taxes play a minor role in investment decisions, and that relatively large changes in relative tax burdens are required to significantly affect investment patterns. However, these results, or those of the mail survey, do not indicate that tax incentives represent poor public policy. That determination requires a weighing of the benefits—in terms of increased income—against the revenue loss.

EVALUATING THE PUBLIC RETURN TO STATE TAX INCENTIVES

When viewed as a public investment, a tax incentive should be provided when its expected return exceeds the return available on alternative investments. To determine the rate of return requires an estimation of the initial investment (the cost of the tax incentive), the annual return (the new income generated), and the probability that the new investment was induced by the tax incentive. This section will use the results of both the mail survey and the econometric investigations to explore the possible rate of return on state investment tax incentives.

Interpreting Results of the Mail Survey

The mail survey provided estimates of the proportion of firms whose location decisions were influenced by state tax incentives. These estimates can be used as part of the evaluation of tax incentives as public investments.

For the average manufacturing firm, each dollar of new investment in depreciable assets generates about $1.44 in annual income, including payroll, profits, and interest payments (see Appendix IV for details on the methods used in this section). This is the relevant stream of benefits to be used in a benefit-cost analysis if all of the new income remains within the state (that is, all employees initially resided in the state, all owners reside in the state, and all lenders are located in the state). The cost—or initial public investment—is the dollar cost of the investment tax credit.

This information can be used to estimate the annual return on the revenue loss. For example, the largest investment tax credit is that of New York at 4 percent. Thus, each dollar of investment in depreciable assets generates a first year, one-time cost of $.04, and a continuing stream of income of $1.44. If all of this new income can be attributed to recipients within the state, the annual rate of return on investment is 3590 percent. Of course, this tremendously exaggerates the value of the tax incentive because it implicitly assumes that all new investment is due solely to the subsidy. The results need to be adjusted to take into account the fact that only a proportion of new investment is actually induced by the incentive. If the public discount rate, or opportunity cost of its funds, is 10 percent, what proportion of the investment needs to have been due to the subsidy for the adjusted return to just equal 10 percent? Only .26 percent of total investment is required to have been affected if 10 percent is the "threshold" rate of return.

However, this example assumes away a number of factors which would serve to increase the proportion of investment affected in order for the tax incentive to be acceptable public investment. First, in many cases it is unlikely that all of the new income—payroll, profits, and interest—should be attributed to the state. Particularly for new branch plants, additional workers are imported from out of state, and owners and lenders are located elsewhere. For the most part, small firms and expansions are more likely to use local labor and be locally owned and financed. Second, a new manufacturing facility may call forth new public investment, such as roads, sewers, or schools, unless there is appropriate underutilized public capacity. If this is the case, the cost of the infrastructure should be added to the direct cost of the tax incentive in evaluating the rate of return. Again, it is more likely that new branch plants will require additional infrastructure than the start-up and expansion of firms in the area will. Third, given the tremendous uncertainty surrounding the actual return to be achieved, the opportunity cost—or discount rate—on the use of public funds should be increased. Just as private investors demand higher returns for risky investments, the public sector should demand higher returns on very uncertain investments. One illustrative set of assumptions about these factors is that half of the income flows out of state or to new immigrants, that infrastructure equal to 25 percent of private depreciable investment is called for, and that uncertainty results in an increase in the discount rate from 10 percent to 20 percent. Under this set of assumptions, the "break-even" probability rises from only .26 percent to 8.1 percent.

This example was based on the largest state tax incentive. A smaller tax incentive would be a desirable public investment at a lower probability of inducing investment because the initial costs are lower. The survey results allow the comparison of states with different levels of subsidy, and while extremely tentative, such a comparison does not indicate that a smaller subsidy reduces the effectiveness in influencing firms. Maintaining the optimistic assumptions that all income remains in-state, that no other public infrastructure is required, and that the discount rate is only 10 percent, the required "break-even" probability drops from .28 percent for the largest tax credit down to only .007 percent for the smallest subsidy. However, with such a small subsidy, any additional public infrastructure completely dominates the calculation of rate of return (because it is equivalent to a 25 percent tax credit in the first year). Under the alternative assumptions of half of the income remaining within the state, an additional 25 percent public infrastructure, and a 20 percent discount rate, the break-even probability increases to 7 percent.

The results clearly indicate that, given equal chances of influencing investment, tax incentives will be a better public investment where there is underutilized public infrastructure, labor, and capital, so that public costs are lower and a higher proportion of income remains within the state. The results from the mail survey indicate actual probabilities of influencing the location of investment somewhat in the required range under the alternative assumptions—3.3 percent of new firms, none of expansions, and 6.3 percent of new branch plants. A final determination of the value of tax incentives must rest on the specific circumstances of each state and the new private investments undertaken. It is possible that tax incentives are appropriate public investments.

Interpreting Results the Econometric Investigtions   A somewhat different approach must be used to examine the return to tax changes using the econometric results. The two measures of state tax burdens on business—TAXLOAD (the actual dollar value of tax burdens) and ORDERST (a measure of the rank of the state for a given industry)—do not incorporate the effect of temporary tax incentives. Instead, the results indicate the level of sensitivity of investment to relative tax burdens among states. The form of the equations—with share of national investment the dependent variable—assumes that interstate tax changes influence the location of investment but not the national total (a constant-sum game). In determining the rate of return to state tax changes from these results, the key measure is the elasticity of investment share with respect to relative tax burden. The elasticity measure can be used to determine the amount of induced investment as a result of a 1 percent change in a state's average tax burden, which can then be used to determine the stream of benefits. The cost in lost revenues is a continuing cost when an overall reduction is used rather than a limited tax incentive.

When TAXLOAD—the absolute dollar amount of average business tax burden—is used in the equation, the only industry showing a statistically significant negative response is Rubber and Miscellaneous

Plastic Products. In that industry, the elasticity of investment share is

.176, indicating that a reduction of 1 percent of average business tax burden should lead to an increase of .176 percent of that state's share of total industry investment. In the Rubber industry, this represents an increase of only $58,930 in new investment (for details of the methodology used in this section, see Appendix IV). With each dollar of new depreciable investment resulting in $1.44 of new income, this results in an annual income increase of $84,623. The cost of this new investment is the 1 percent reduction in tax revenues applied to all the new Rubber investment (note that applying the reduction to all new investment is still far more targeted than applying to all Rubber business income). This represents an annual loss of about $30,135. Thus, new income exceeds annual costs, and the annual return is about 281 percent. Even if it is assumed that only half of the new income can be attributed to the state, and that additional public infrastructure is required (equal to 25 percent of the induced new investment), the annual return is still far above the 20 percent required for a risky public investment.

However, these results hold only if the general tax reduction can be targeted solely to the Rubber industry. No other industry exhibited a significant negative response to tax burdens as measured by TAXLOAD. Unless the tax reduction was targeted, all new manufacturing investment would receive the reduction, substantially increasing the lost revenue but not increasing the amount of new investment. Rubber and Miscellaneous Plastics accounted for only 3.8 percent of overall manufacturing investment in 1977. If only the new Rubber investment produced new income, this would reduce the rate of return substantially. With all income assumed to remain within the state, the return would drop to 10.7 percent, or only 5.4 percent if half of the income remained within the state. It would drop even more if additional public infrastructure was required. Using 20 percent as the desired return on public investments with uncertain return, across-the-board reductions in the tax burden on new manufacturing investment are not acceptable public investments. For each state, the actual returns would depend on the mix of new investment. In states where the Rubber industry is significantly larger than the national average, an across-the-board reduction may be an acceptable public investment. In states where it is less than the national average, the returns will be quite small and sometimes negative.

It is more difficult to interpret the econometric results based on equations containing ORDERST as a measure of business tax burden, because ORDERST represents a ranking of state tax burdens rather than the actual taxes paid. Thus, any estimates of elasticity of investment share represent the response to a change in the order statistic of 1 percent and not a change in the business tax burden. However, it is possible to make some reasonable assumptions and interpret the results, although they should be treated with the greatest of caution.

With about fifty states in the ranking, and if the amount of difference between each state was approximately equal, a change of 1 percent in the order statistic would correspond to about half of a rank change. Since there would be a 100 percent change from the lowest to highest state in the ranking, this change of half of a rank would correspond to a 1 percent change in the underlying tax burden if the ranks are fairly evenly distributed.

ORDERST, as a measure of tax burden, resulted in slightly better results than TAXLOAD—a significant coefficients in five industries and slightly higher R^2 values. For Chemicals, Petroleum, Rubber, and Fabricated Metals, negative elasticities of -.020, -.013, -.004, and -.002, respectively, were estimated. These are substantially lower than the estimates found using TAXLOAD. For the highest elasticity— Chemicals—the annual gain in new income is substantially less than the annual loss in tax revenue from a 1 percent reduction in tax burden, even with the most optimistic assumptions about the distribution of new income and the need for public infrastructure investment. For lower elasticity industries, including Rubber, the disparities between new income and lost revenues increase. Thus, the results using ORDERST indicate that even targeted reductions in business taxes are inappropriate. Untargeted reductions to new manufacturing investment would fare extremely poorly.

Summary of the Public Return Discussion A clear-cut conclusion on the value of business tax reductions is not possible given this evidence. For states with very small tax incentives, only a tiny fraction of new investment needs to have been induced for the incentive to have been an appropriate public investment. For states with the largest tax incentives, the required proportion of induced investment, given reasonable assumptions about the distribution of income, the public discount rate, and the need for new infrastructure investment, lies in the general range found from the survey results. Further clarification requires much more detailed information on the hiring and ownership structures of firms receiving incentives, as well as on their need for supporting public infrastructure.

The regression results point to a more clear-cut conclusion. Given the estimates of the elasticity of investment share with respect to overall tax changes, untargeted business tax reductions are very poor public investments even if applied only to new investment. In only one industry—the Rubber industry—and with one of the two measures of tax burden, the evidence indicates that a targeted reduction in business taxes would be an appropriate public investment. Using the alternative measure, even targeting tax reductions to those sectors where a significant effect on investment was detected is found to be inappropriate.

SUMMARY OF THE RESULTS OF THE NEW EMPIRICAL RESEARCH

A substantial amount of progress has been made in the research reported in this chapter toward resolving some of the issues surrounding the value of state tax incentives. While methodological problems dictate that caution is required in interpreting the results, the most important conclusions of the research include the following:

- The initial foregone revenues for states, taken as a whole, are substantial, and deserving of evaluation.
- Most firms making new investments do not even consider locating in any state other than their final choice.
- Most firms making new investments in states with tax incentives are unaware that the incentives exist.
- Only a very small proportion of firms making investments claim that they would have located in another state in the absence of tax incentives.
- In most industries, the general level of business taxation has an undetectable effect on investment patterns.
- In those industries where an effect can be detected, it is quite small.
- When evaluated as a public investment, specific tax incentives may have an acceptable rate of return, particularly if targeted to areas of high unemployment and unused public infrastructure.
- Overall business tax reductions, even if targeted to sensitive industries, do not appear to be acceptable state tax policy for stimulating investment.

5

A GUIDE FOR THE PERPLEXED: POLICY DIRECTIONS

In a great many choices faced by public policymakers, reasonably careful analytical work is unable to transform messy, confused issues into simple, clear cut choices between "good" and "bad" public policy. The issue of state tax incentives, and the analysis contained in this study, is not an exception. In such cases, empirical work should strive to eliminate extreme claims, and leave the tough choices to political figures.

Two extreme claims should be immediately discarded. First, it is not true, as some have claimed, that business tax incentives influence a substantial number of firms to locate in a given state. Second, it is also false that no firms are influenced by tax incentives or interstate tax differentials. Tax incentives do appear to influence some firms, but very few. For the great majority, the reduced taxes represent a pleasant windfall. Given the small size of most state tax incentives, it is probably true that some of the firms who changed their location due to the subsidy made an irrational decision.

There appear to be two quite distinct strategies open to states which choose to employ tax incentives. First, states can assume that the incentives are generally ineffectual, but are indicative of the state's interest in new business development. Alternatively, they can assume that sufficiently large subsidies do influence some firms and should be designed to reduce the number of windfalls. The adoption of either strategy leads to quite different use of incentives. In either case, the results of the mail survey, which found substantial differences among new firms, expansions, and new branch plants, should influence the final subsidy strategy.

THE "CHEAP" SIGNALING STRATEGY

For the state which assumes that tax incentives are quite weak in their ability to influence location decisions, but act to either influence the seriousness of the search process or simply fool some irrational firms, the smallest possible incentives should be employed. This seems to be the strategy of those states offering incentives as small as $50 per $100,000 investment. It is quite difficult to construct scenarios in which such a small incentive could act to offset tax or nontax differentials among competing states. Its only purpose can be to cause those firms which look to alternative states to more seriously investigate those with tax incentives, or to make business decisionmakers feel wanted. In these cases, the tax incentives should probably be widely advertised among out-of-state firms. The availability of the tax incentive, in practice, should be limited by imposing minimum investment or employment requirements. The combined strategy of advertising plus minimum size requirements will increase the information value of the incentive while severely restricting the revenue loss. Such small incentives should then be evaluated relative to other advertising and outreach strategies rather than on the basis of their ability to directly influence location decisions.

THE SERIOUS SUBSIDY APPROACH For those states which choose to take tax incentives as a direct means of seriously influencing location, the study contains a number of important policy conclusions. First, incentives appear to affect a larger proportion of investments made by new firms and new branch plants than by new expansions. Second, the effect of taxes on the share of investment appears to vary among industries, with Rubber, Chemicals, Petroleum, and Fabricated Metal Products more responsive than other sectors. Third, benefit-cost studies indicate that the return on the subsidies is higher if local residents and capital sources are used in the project, and if underutilized public infrastructure can be used. Such conditions are more likely to be attained if new firms and expansions, rather than out-of-state branch plants, are subsidized.

These considerations indicate that it may be very desirable to target tax incentives to firms whose characteristics indicate responsiveness and to areas of labor pools whose nature serves to increase the public rate of return. Such a targeted approach is certain to be more appropriate than an across-the-board reduction in business taxes and probably more attractive than tax incentives available to all new investment. Given that targeting is desirable, a classical choice in public policy arises: the use of legislative change in the tax code to provide automatic tax incentives to all firms which meet certain criteria versus administrative selection of investment projects to receive tax incentives or direct grants. The former method—automatic tax incentives—substantially reduces the public overhead cost of maintaining a staff to make individual determinations, but almost certainly acts to increase the proportion of subsidies which are windfalls to recipients.

Some states already provide targeted incentives through existing tax codes. For example, Oregon provides tax incentives to manufacturing firms locating in depressed areas. Maine limits its tax incentives to firms undertaking quite large investments (so much so that to date only one firm has taken advantage of the subsidy). The Commerce Clearing

House *State Tax Review* frequently reports special exemptions from sales taxes or a portion of property taxes for very specific industries in some states. However, it is not clear that these forms of targeting are the most appropriate. It is unlikely that simple geographical criteria—such as unemployment rate in a country—are sufficient to ensure that firms investing in lagging areas primarily hire local residents, or rely upon surplus public infrastructure. In some states, targeting the stage of investment—whether new firms, expansions, or new branch plants—may be unconstitutional on the basis of discriminating among forms of investment. Finally, targeting tax incentives to specific industries through legislation should require constant fine tuning and has the potential to reflect political influence rather than expected return on a public investment. In addition to these general problems, the temptation to target tightly through an inflexible tax code should be partially constrained by the realization that some firms outside of targeted areas, targeted sectors, or targeted stage of investment may be influenced by the incentives and provide net benefits. If incentives are provided through the tax code on an automatic basis, a reasonable case can be made for not targeting them.

The alternative subsidy device is to provide public employees with the discretion to provide cash grants or negotiated incentives to firms making new investments. This approach is widely pursued in Europe, and has parallels in the United States in the Urban Development Action Grant (UDAG) program and the formal and informal ability of some local tax assessors and city councils to provide negotiated reductions in property tax rates.

In theory, public officials should make case-by-case determinations on the likely net benefits of each subsidy. This would include judgments about whether the firm would have made the investment without the subsidy. To increase net benefits, subsidies might be made contingent on hiring local unemployed workers or locating in areas with underutilized public infrastructure. The level of subsidy could vary from case to case, reflecting judgments about the level needed to influence a location decision and the magnitude of net benefits from the investment (in contrast, all automatic tax incentives are mandated as a certain percent of eligible investment or wages). Where cash grants are made, ideally the development officials will seek to maximize the net benefits given the annual allocation of funding.

The discretionary grants are simultaneously more subject to public oversight and less desirable political influence than automatic tax incentives are. They will be subject to annual budget review and are exercised at the discretion of development officials rather than private investors. However, depending on the level of independence of the negotiators, they can also be held hostage by legislators seeking subsidies for constituents.

The relative attractiveness of discretionary incentives depends largely on the ability of the public negotiators to determine whether or not an investment would have been made in any case. If a substantial number of windfall subsidies can be eliminated, the discretionary program is probably a superior policy. If sufficient discrimination is not possible, the program will serve to provide subsidies to firms with superior political influence and the ability to penetrate the inevitable obstacle course of applications and hearings.

For those states which choose to provide subsidies, it may be desirable to provide both an automatic and a discretionary subsidy program. The automatic subsidy would be quite small, but heavily advertised to out-of-state firms. The discretionary subsidies would be budgeted each year, with each award subject to legislative veto. Negotiators would have broad flexibility in choosing firms and projects, including the ability to impose both hiring and location requirements.

CONCLUSIONS

The preceding remarks should not be interpreted as support for the provision of tax incentives. To the contrary, in many ways the provision of tax incentives represents a significant obstacle to sound development policy. Even if tax incentives are a good public investment, meeting the conditions discussed in Chapter Four, they will influence only a tiny proportion of new investment in any state. While the evidence is unclear about whether or not targeted incentives are a *good* policy, it is unequivocal about whether or not incentives are a *significant* policy. They are not. The evidence provides little support for those who believe that poor states, or stagnating states, can stimulate their economies in any significant way by a heavy reliance on either targeted tax incentives or across the board reductions in business taxes. Even where the evidence indicates that incentives are potentially a good public investment, they could be eliminated with almost an unnoticeable effect on a state's economy. In contrast, if the amount of time state legislatures spend debating tax incentives and the effect of taxes on investment was redirected toward other areas, substantial progress might be made. Tax incentives are clearly not a substitute for state initiatives in labor markets, capital markets, transportation, regulation, and the quality of life. Too often it is easier to pass a tax incentive, and widely advertise it, than to deal with more fundamental problems. To ignore the problems and factors which influence the great majority of investment decisions is to doom a state's development policy to marginal influence.

BIBLIOGRAPHY

1. Advisory Commission on Intergovernmental Relations (1980). "Regional Growth: Interstate Tax Competition," Report A–76 (Washington, D.C.)

2. Advisory Commission on Intergovernmental Relations (1980). *Significant Features of Fiscal Federalism:* 1979–1980 Edition. Report M–123 (Washington, D.C.).

3. Birch, D. (1979). *The Job Generation Process.* MIT Program on Neighborhood and Regional Change, Cambridge, Massachusetts.

4. Buchanan, J. and Moes, J. (1960). "A Regional Countermeasure to the Minimum Wage," *American Economic Review,* June.

5. Campbell, A. (1965). "State and Local Taxes, Expenditures, and Economic Development," in *State and Local Taxes on Business,* Tax Institute of America (Princeton, New Jersey).

6. Carlton, D. (1979). "Why New Firms Locate Where They Do: An Econometric Model," Working Paper Number 57, Joint Center for Urban Studies of MIT and Harvard (Cambridge, Massachusetts).

7. Cornia, G., Testa, A., and Stocker, F. (1978). "State-Local Fiscal Incentives and Economic Development," Urban and Regional Development Series Paper Number 4, Academy for Contemporary Problems (Columbus, Ohio).

8. Daniels, B. and Kieschnick, M. (1979). *Development Finance: A Primer for Policymakers.* The National Rural Center (Washington, D.C.).

9. Dorgan, B. (1980). "North Dakota's New Industry Tax Exemption: Economic Incentive or Tax Giveaway," A Study for Presentation to the State Board of Equalization and the North Dakota State Legislature, North Dakota State Tax Commission (Fargo, North Dakota).

10. Genetski, R. and Chin, Y. (1978). "The Impact of State and Local Taxes on Economic Growth," *Harris Economic Research Office Service,* Harris Bank (Chicago, Illinois).

11. Harrison, B. and Kanter, S. (1978). "The Political Economy of State Job Creation Incentives," *Journal of the American Institute of Planners,* October.

12. Hodge, J. (1978). "A Study of Industries' Regional Investment Decisions," unpublished paper, Federal Reserve Bank of New York (New York, New York).

13. *Inc.* Magazine (1980). "Buildings and Site Selection" (Boston, Massachusetts).

14. Jusenius, C. and Ledebur, L. (1977). "The Migration of Firms and Workers in Ohio: 1970-1975," Academy for Contemporary Problems (Columbus, Ohio).

15. Kanter, S. (1977). "Another Look at State Business Subsidies," a paper presented at the Seventieth Annual Conference on Taxation, National Tax Association-Tax Institute of America.

16. Moes, J. (1961). *Local Subsidies for Industry.* University of North Carolina Press (Chapel Hill, North Carolina).

17. McMillan, T. (1969). "Why Manufacturers Choose Plant Locations Versus Determinants of Plant Locations," *Land Economics,* August.

18. Morgan, W. (1964). "The Effects of State and Local Taxes and Financial Inducements on Industrial Location," unpublished PhD dissertation at the University of Colorado.

19. Morgan, W. and Hackbart, M. (1974). "An Analysis of State and Local Industrial Tax Exemption Programs," *Southern Economic Journal,* October.

20. Mueller, E. and Morgan, J. (1962). "Location Decisions of Manufacturers," Papers and Proceedings of the 74th Annual Meeting of the American Economics Association.

21. Oster, S. (1979). "Industrial Search for New Locations: An Empirical Analysis," *Review of Economics and Statistics,* May.

22. Price Waterhouse & Co. (1978). *State Tax Comparison Study* (St. Louis, Missouri).

23. Reigeluth, G., Wolman, H. and Reinhard, R. (1979). "The Fiscal Consequences of Changes in a Community's Economic Base: A Review of the Literature," The Urban Institute (Washington, D.C.).

24. Rinehart, J. (1962). "Rates of Return on Municipal Subsidies to Industries," an unpublished PhD dissertation, University of Virginia.

25. Rinehart, J. and Laird, W. (1972). "Community Inducements to Industry and the Zero Sum Game," *Scottish Journal of Political Economy,* February.

26. Ross, W. (1953). "Tax Exemption in Louisiana as a Device for Encouraging Industrial Development," *The Southwestern Social Science Quarterly,* February-March.

27. Sacks, S. (1965). "State and Local Finances and Economic Development," in *State and Local Taxes on Business,* Tax Institute of America (Princeton, New Jersey).

28. Schmenner, R. (1978). "The Manufacturing Location Decision: Evidence from Cincinnati and New England," a paper prepared for the Economic Development Administration, (Washington, D.C.).

29. Stafford, H. (1974). "The Anatomy of the Location Decision: Content Analysis of Case Studies," in *Spatial Perspectives on Industrial Organization and Decision-making,* ed. F.E. Ian Hamilton (John Wiley, New York).

30. Struyk, R. (1967). "An Analysis of Tax Structure, Public Service Levels, and Regional Economic Growth," *Journal of Regional Science,* Winter.

31. Thompson, W. and Mattila, J. (1959). *An Econometric Model of Postwar State Industrial Development,* Wayne State University Press (Detroit, Michigan).

32. Vasquez, T. and deSeve, C. (1977). "State/Local Taxes and Juridictional Shifts in Corporate Business Activity: The Complications of Measurement," *National Tax Journal,* September.

33. Vaughan, R. (1977). *The Urban Impacts of Federal Policies: Volume 2, Economic Development.* R–2028–KF/RC. The Rand Corporation (Washington, D.C.).

34. Vaughan, R. (1980). Abscam paper, unpublished.

35. Williams, W. (1967). "A Measure of the Impact of State and Local Taxes on Industry Location," *Journal of Regional Science,* Summer.

36. Wolman, H. (1979). "Components of Employment Change: A Review of the Literature," The Urban Institute (Washington, D.C.).

37. Zubrow, R. (1961). "Some Difficulties with the Measurement of Comparative Tax Burdens," National Tax Association Proceedings, 54th Annual Conference.

APPENDIX I

METHODOLOGY FOR CALCULATING STATE AND LOCAL TAX BURDENS ON BUSINESS

This appendix provides an explanation of the methods used to calculate the tax burdens displayed in Table 5. The most important point to understand is that the taxes are calculated on the basis of *hypothetical* balance sheets and income statements—not those of specific corporations operating in each state. For the All Manufacturing category, the following financial figures were used:

Balance Sheet		Income Statement	
Total Assets	$8,728,000	Sales	$6,919,920
Inventory	1,803,000	Operating Income	958,560
Machinery and			
Equipment	1,974,400		
Plant and Structures	693,680		
Land	354,000		
Capital Stock	1,065,000		
Retained Earnings	3,354,000		

These figures were derived largely from the Federal Trade Commission's *Quarterly Financial Report.* Each quarter, the FTC reports the total balance sheet and income statement for the U.S. manufacturing sector. To arrive at financial information for an average firm, the 1979 Third Quarter results were divided by the number of manufacturing corporations reporting income to the Internal Revenue Service in 1974 (the last year available from the IRS). The third quarter of 1979 was used to avoid distortions due to the 1980 recession.

To arrive at the tax burden for each state, the tax rates of each state (as reported in the *All States Handbook* published by Prentice-Hall) were applied to the hypothetical corporation. The only taxes considered were property taxes, corporate income or franchise taxes, capital value taxes, and sales taxes on purchases by manufacturing firms. In the case of property taxes, the average rate reported by Prentice-Hall was used, although this necessarily ignores a good deal of intrastate variation in some cases. Not included in the comparison were unemployment insurance or workmen compensation taxes, which do vary among states, but are largely experience rated, making it almost impossible to provide reasonable estimates of interstate differences. For purposes of simplicity and to avoid problems of allocating income among states, it was assumed that all assets, employees, and sales of the firm occur within the state in question. The results should be interpreted as representing the taxes paid by a firm in different states, with the firm in question operating in some state—not in its initial years. This allows special tax credits to be ignored. For the most part, such credits are very small, and only apply early in the life of a particular investment or hiring expansion.

Similar results were obtained for thirteen other industry classifications, and are available from the author. The same methodology was used to calculate state and local tax burdens for 1977, which were used in the investment equations discussed in Chapter Four. These results are also available from the author.

APPENDIX II

METHODOLOGY AND DETAILS ON THE MAIL SURVEY

DESCRIPTION OF METHODOLOGY All corporations surveyed had actually made a manufacturing investment in 1979. Only firms which had invested in a state which automatically offers, through its tax code, specific investment and or employment incentives, were included in the sample. These states were New York, Massachusetts, Montana, Kansas, Delaware, New Mexico, Colorado, Rhode Island, West Virginia, Maine, and North Dakota. Because the filing date for tax returns in these states had already passed at the time of the survey, it is likely that the tax incentive had already been exercised unless the firm was not profitable and had no state tax liability.

Three different kinds of manufacturing investment decisions were analyzed through the surveys: the creation of a new company, the creation of a new branch plant of an existing company, and the expansion of an existing plant. The identities of companies for the survey were obtained from two sources. For new companies, a listing of all manufacturing companies established during 1979 in the eleven states was purchased from Dun and Bradstreet, which maintains such records for credit-rating and marketing purposes. For the new branch plants and expansions, listings were taken from 1979 issues of *Industrial Development* magazine, published by the Industrial Development Research Council, which attempts to identify and publish all investments in excess of $500,000.

Determining the appropriate recipient of the survey is quite important, since the ideal respondent would have participated directly in the decision and have been in a position to have weighed a variety of factors in choosing. For the new companies, this represented no obstacle, since the records purchased form Dun and Bradstreet included the name of the president of the firm, and all of the companies involved were extremely small. For the branch plants and expansions, however, considerable difficulties were involved. There is a great deal of variation among large firms in the way in which they organizationally structure the decision about plant location and expansion. *Industrial Development* periodically surveys corporations **93** to identify the executive in charge of process, and publishes the results. When identified for the companies in the sample, these executives were used. When not identified, the next alternative, for publicly held corporations, involved obtaining a recent annual report and attempting to identify an executive with the title of vice-president for facility planning, real estate, or corporate planning. If not available, the chief executive officer was used. For firms which were not publicly held, the headquarters of the company was telephoned, and a name obtained.

RESULTS FOR NEW COMPANIES   Surveys were sent to all of the 1,821 new companies identified in the Dun and Brad street files. Seventy six were returned unopened, usually labeled "Moved—no forwarding address" by the Postal Service. A reasonable assumption is that these firms had failed after they were entered in the Dun and Bradstreet file. A significant number of new firms are undoubtedly not in the data base yet. However, almost all firms seeking outside credit from suppliers or lenders would be in the file. It is reasonable to assume that those excluded were generally smaller and operated largely on a cash/personal checking account basis. Such firms are probably less sophisticated in many aspects of business decisionmaking, and less likely to have considered a location in another state.

Three hundred and thirty-seven usable survey forms were returned. This is a response rate of 19.3 percent among the sample, taking out those returned by the Postal Service. Table 2-1 compares the distribution of responses with the sample in terms of state of origin, while Table 2-2 compares the distribution of responses with the sample in terms of two-digit SIC classification.

Interpretation of Relative Importance of Location Factors for New Firms   Table 22 in the text presents the results of the survey question asking about the relative importance of differences among states in making location choices. There are a number of ways to interpret such survey answers. A number of ways of ranking the importance of the various factors are shown in Table 2-3 below. The first column focuses solely on those factors mentioned most frequently as a deciding positive influence. This method, however, completely discards the information that is contained in the other answers. Thus, the second column simply adds the responses of those who found a factor of deciding importance and those who found it of moderate positive influence. Another way to combine these two answers is shown in the third column, where those who rank a factor of deciding positive influence receive double the weight of those who rate a factor of

Table 2-1

Distribution of Sample and Responses by State: New Firms

State	Sample Number	Sample Percent	Responses Number	Percent of Responses	Response Rate
New York	906	49.8%	131	38.9%	14.5%
Delaware	25	1.4	9	2.7	36.0
Colorado	227	12.5	59	17.5	26.0
New Mexico	33	1.8	5	1.5	15.2
Montana	45	2.5	10	3.0	22.2
Massachusetts	303	16.6	61	18.1	20.1
Kansas	105	5.8	23	6.8	21.9
Rhode Island	119	6.5	27	8.0	22.7
West Virginia	38	2.1	9	2.7	18.4
North Dakota	20	1.1	3	.9	15.0
	1,821		337		

The Chi-square test for differences between the distribution by state for the responses and the sample indicates that the responses differ significantly from the sample. The primary difference between the responses and the sample is the underrepresentation of new companies from New York and the overrepresentation of new companies from Colorado.

moderate positive influence. The fourth column is the ranking of factors found to be a moderate negative influence.

While there is no single correct way of interpreting the results, there is substantial consistency in the different rankings. With all five methods, access to current customers, access to a growing market, and personal reasons of management are the top three factors. With the exception of the inverse negative ranking, the least important factors are political climate, the supply of fuel and electricity, the cost of fuel and electricity, and air quality regulations. The two tax factors are consistently in the lower half of the rankings (except for the negative ranking).

SELECTED RESULTS FOR EXPANSION INVESTMENTS

As noted in the text, expansion investments in eligible states were identified through various issues of *Industrial Development*. Surveys were sent to firms which had made 143 expansion investments. Usable survey results were received from fifty firms, for an overall response rate of 35 percent. One letter was received from a firm which had made four separate expansion investments in 1979, and chose to describe the factors relevant to those investments without using the

Table 2-2

Distribution of Sample and Responses by Sector: New Firms

Sector	Sample Number	Sample Percent	Responses Number	Percent of Responses	Response Rate
20	94	4.2%	18	5.3%	19.1%
21	1	.1	0	0	0
22	68	3.7	8	2.4	11.8
23	290	15.9	25	7.4	8.6
24	110	6.0	19	5.6	17.3
25	82	4.5	17	5.0	20.7
26	36	2.0	6	1.8	16.7
28	58	3.2	14	4.2	24.1
29	6	.3	1	.3	16.7
30	72	4.0	13	3.9	18.1
31	41	2.3	8	2.4	19.5
32	67	3.7	18	5.3	26.9
33	40	2.2	7	2.1	17.5
34	204	11.2	52	15.4	25.5
35	256	14.1	56	16.6	21.9
36	111	6.1	21	6.2	18.9
37	0	0	0	0	0
38	76	4.2	21	6.2	27.6
39	209	11.5	33	9.8	15.8
	1,821		**337**		

The Chi-square with eighteen degrees of freedom is 33.13, indicating that the response distribution is significantly different than the sample distribution. This largely reflects the underrepresentation of Sector 23 (the Apparel industry), and the overrepresentation of Sectors 32 (Stone, Clay, and Glass) and 38 (Instruments). Because Sector 23 is heavily concentrated in New York, the primary distortion appears to be due to the low response rate from the New York City Apparel industry, which is well known for its dependence on illegal aliens and attempts to avoid any public probing.

---

survey form. The pattern of response is compared to the pattern of the sample in terms of geographical and sectoral distribution in Tables 2-4 and 2-5 below.

Interpretation of Relative Importance of Location Factors for Expansions Table 2-6 uses a number of ways to interpret the survey responses from expansion firms. As with the new firms, the most important location factors are identified consistently through any of the ranking methods, with economies of scale, maintaining an intact labor force, the ease of expanding on-site, and access to raw materials consistently the most influential. After the top four, the rankings are much less consistent, largely reflecting the volatility of a ranking procedure when

Table 2-3

Ranking of the Importance of Location Factors for New Firms

FACTORS	Deciding Mentions	Deciding + Moderate	Deciding + .5 Moderate	Inverse Negative Ranking
Access to current customers	1	1	1	1
Access to growing market	2	2	2	2
Personal reasons	3	3	3	3
Access to raw materials	4	8	5	11
Availability of capital	5	7	6	6
Familiarity with economy	6	4	4	4
Supply of skilled labor	7	6	8	5
Transportation	8	5	7	10
Land costs	9	14	12	15
Costs of skilled labor	10	9	9	7
Personal taxes	11	15	14	20
Cost of unskilled labor	12	12	13	12
Business taxes	13	11	10	19
Supply of unskilled labor	14	10	11	8
Union activities	15	16	16	18
Climate	16	13	15	13
Political climate	17	19	18	17
Supply fuel/electricity	18	17	17	9
Cost of fuel/electricity	19	18	19	14
Air quality	20	20	20	16

SOURCE: derived from Table 22

Table 2-4

Distribution of Sample and Responses by State: Expansions

State	Sample Number	Sample Percent	Responses Number	Percent of Responses	Response Rate
New York	41	28.7%	10	20.0%	24.4%
Delaware	4	2.8	1	2.0	25.0
Colorado	11	7.7	5	10.0	45.4
New Mexico	3	2.1	2	4.0	66.7
Montana	0	0	0	0	0
Massachusetts	32	22.4	10	20.0	31.3
Kansas	26	18.2	13	26.0	50.0
Rhode Island	8	5.6	4	8.0	50.0
Maine	3	2.1	2	4.0	66.7
West Virginia	15	10.5	3	5.6	20.0
North Dakota	0	0	0	0	0
Total	**143**		**50**		**35.0%**

Table 2-5

Distribution of Sample and Responses by Sector: Expansions

Sector	Sample		Responses		
	Number	Percent	Number	Percent of Responses	Response Rate
20	8	5.6%	1	2.0%	0.0%
21	0	0.0	0	0	0.0
22	1	0.7	1	2.0	100.0
23	2	1.4	1	2.0	50.0
24	1	0.7	0	0.0	0.0
25	0	0.0	0	0.0	0.0
26	5	3.5	3	6.0	60.0
28	14	9.8	3	6.0	21.4
29	4	2.8	2	4.0	50.0
30	8	5.6	2	4.0	25.0
31	2	1.4	2	4.0	100.0
32	1	0.7	0	0.0	0.0
33	7	4.9	1	2.0	14.3
34	8	5.6	6	12.0	75.0
35	18	12.6	6	12.0	33.3
36	18	12.6	8	16.0	44.4
37	7	4.9	6	12.0	85.7
38	6	4.2	2	4.0	33.3
39	1	0.7	1	2.0	100.0
Unidentified	32	22.4	5	10.0	15.6
Total	**143**		**50**		**35.0%**

The Chi-square test indicates that the responses differ significantly from the sample in both the distribution of firms by state and sector. The Chi-square is relatively smaller for the distribution by states, and primarily reflects underrepresentation of New York and overrepresentation of Kansas, Maine, and New Mexico. The distribution by sector is distorted primarily by overrepresentation in SIC 37 (Transportation) where six of the seven firms in the sample responded, SIC 34 (Fabricated Metal Products), and significant underrepresentation among firms whose SIC could not be identified.

---

there are relatively few responses (so that a shift of one or two answers can move a ranking several places).

SELECTED RESULTS FOR NEW BRANCH PLANTS New branch plants, as parts of existing firms, were selected from listings in *Industrial Development*. It is possible that a very small number of new branch plants were actually new firms with an initial investment of over $500,000. However, there was no overlap between firms identified as new companies through the Dun and Bradstreet listings and those identified as new branch plants by *Industrial Development*. Survey forms were sent to 101 new plants.

Table 2-6

Ranking of Importance of Location Factors for Expansions

FACTORS	# Deciding	Deciding + Moderate	Deciding + .5 Moderate	Inverse Negative
Economies of scale	1	4	3	12
Maintain labor	1	1	1	1
Ease of expanding	1	2	2	1
Raw materials	4	4	4	1
Present customers	4	6	6	1
Political climate	4	18	12	20
Personal reasons	4	10	7	12
Growing market	7	13	12	1
Supply of fuel	7	13	12	16
Union activities	7	18	15	24
Supply skilled	7	2	4	1
Capital	7	10	8	1
Cost skilled labor	13	6	8	16
Cost of fuel	13	13	15	20
Product line	13	6	8	12
Transportation	13	6	8	1
Personal taxes	18	18	17	20
Supply unskilled	18	18	21	12
Cost unskilled	18	13	17	16
Climate	18	18	21	1
Familiarity	18	23	23	1
Land costs	18	13	17	16
Air regulation	23	23	24	1
Business taxes	24	10	17	20

SOURCE: Derived from responses in Table 23

Usable responses were received from thirty two firms, a response rate of 31.7 percent. The distribution of the sample and the responses by state and sector are displayed in Tables 2-7 and 2-8 below.

Interpretation of Relative Importance of Location Factors for New Branch Plants As with the new firms and expansion investments, it is possible to interpret the answers to the survey question about the relative importance of interstate differences in a number of ways. As shown in Table 2-9 below, the supply of skilled labor is consistently ranked as the first or second most important factor by all methods. When the number of "deciding" and "moderate" mentions are added together, the cost of skilled labor becomes the most important factor. Business taxes are generally considered fairly important with each method. Overall, those factors ranked in the first half of the rankings by one method are in the first half in the other rankings, with the significant

Table 2-7

Distribution of Sample and Responses by State: New Plants

State	Sample Number	Sample Percent	Responses Number	Percent of Responses	Response Rate
New York	40	39.6%	11	34.4%	27.5%
Delaware	8	7.9	0	0.0	0.0
Colorado	10	9.9	3	9.4	30.0
New Mexico	3	3.0	0	0.0	0.0
Montana	2	2.0	2	6.3	100.0
Massachusetts	9	8.9	3	9.4	33.3
Kansas	14	13.9	8	25.0	57.1
Rhode Island	10	9.9	2	6.3	20.0
Maine	3	3.0	2	6.3	66.7
West Virginia	2	2.0	1	3.1	50.0
North Dakota	0	0.0	0	0.0	0.0
Total	**101**		**32**		**31.7%**

The Chi-square test indicates that the response is significantly different than the sample. This primarily reflects underrepresentation of Delaware and New Mexico, and overrepresentation of Kansas.

exception of the "inverse negative" ranking, in which union activities are frequently mentioned. As with the expansion investments, these rankings are quite sensitive to the shift of even a single firm's answers, given the relatively small number of responses.

Table 2-8

Distribution of Sample and Responses by Sector: New Plants

Sector	Sample Number	Sample Percent	Responses Number	Percent of Responses	Response Rate
20	9	8.9	0	0.0	0.0
21	0	0.0	0	0.0	0.0
22	0	0.0	0	0.0	0.0
23	3	3.0	0	0.0	0.0
24	1	1.0	0	0.0	0.0
25	3	3.0	2	6.3	66.7
26	1	1.0	0	0.0	0.0
28	2	2.0	0	0.0	0.0
29	5	5.0	2	6.3	40.0
30	9	8.9	2	6.3	22.2
31	1	1.0	1	3.1	100.0
32	2	2.0	0	0.0	0.0
33	4	4.0	0	0.0	0.0
34	5	5.0	0	0.0	0.0
35	13	12.9	10	31.3	76.9
36	8	7.9	3	9.4	37.6
37	7	6.9	3	9.4	42.9
38	2	2.0	0	0.0	0.0
39	6	5.9	2	6.3	33.3
Unidentified	20	19.8	7	21.9	35.0
Total	**101**		**32**		**31.7**

The Chi-square test indicates that the distribution of responses is significantly different than the distribution of the sample.

Table 2-9

Ranking of the Importance of Location Factors for New Branch Plants

FACTORS	Deciding	Deciding + Moderate	Deciding + .5 Moderate	Inverse Negative
Supply of skilled labor	1	2	1	1
Supply of unskilled labor	2	9	6	1
Union activities	2	6	3	18
Business taxes	2	9	6	1
Personal reasons	5	4	3	1
Transportation	5	6	6	1
Raw materials access	7	6	10	1
Political climate	7	9	11	10
Cost skilled labor	7	1	2	10
Land costs	7	4	6	1
Capital availability	7	3	3	1
Present customers	12	9	12	10
Growing market	12	18	16	10
Cost of fuel	12	14	14	10
Supply of fuel	12	9	12	1
Cost unskilled labor	16	14	15	10
Climate	16	18	18	18
Personal taxes	16	16	16	20
Familiarity w/economy	19	16	18	1
Air quality regulation	19	18	20	1

SOURCE: Derived from Table 24.

COUNCIL OF STATE PLANNING AGENCIES LOCATION SURVEY
CONFIDENTIAL

In answering the questions in this survey, please refer only to the circumstances relevant in choosing the location for your recent new plant.

1. Did you seriously consider locating this new plant in any other state? Yes ___ No ___ (If you answered "No", please skip question 2 and go on to question 3, 4, and 5.)

2. In choosing among states, please think about the factors which led you to choose your final choice. Focus on *differences* between the state you actually chose and those you considered. For example, if *all* of the states you considered had an ample supply of skilled labor, then this had a insignificant effect in choosing between states. Please look over the list of factors below, and indicate how they influenced you by checking the appropriate column.

Factor	Deciding Positive Influence	Moderate Positive Influence	Insignificant Influence	Moderate Negative Influence
Availability of capital				
Supply of skilled labor				
Costs of skilled labor				
Supply of unskilled labor				
Cost of unskilled labor				
Union activities				
Supply of fuel and electricity				
Cost of fuel and electricity				
Climate				
Personal reasons of management				
Transportation network				
Political climate				
Familiarity with economy				
Air quality regulation				
Business tax structure				
Personal tax structure				
Access to raw materials				
Access to present customers				

(Continued on following page) **103**

Access to growing market
Land costs

3. Some states offer special tax incentives—such as investment tax credits—for new and expanding firms. Did the state tax code of your final choice include a special tax incentive?
Yes __ No __ Don't Know __
If such an incentive was available, please consider the effect of this tax incentive on your location decision.
4. If the tax incentive was *not* offered, would you have located your new plant in another state?
Yes __ No __
5. Without the tax incentive, would you have reduced the *amount* of your investment?
Yes __ No __
Please return to: Council of State Planning Agencies

COUNCIL OF STATE PLANNING AGENCIES LOCATION SURVEY
CONFIDENTIAL

In answering the questions in this survey, please refer only to the circumstances relevant in choosing the location for your recent business start-up.

1. Did you seriously consider locating this new business in any other state? Yes __ No __ (If you answered "No", please skip question 2 and go on to question 3, 4, and 5.)

2. In choosing among states, please think about the factors which led you to choose your final choice. Focus on *differences* between the state you actually chose and those you considered. For example, if *all* of the states you considered had an ample supply of skilled labor, then this had a insignificant effect in choosing between states. Please look over the list of factors below, and indicate how they influenced you by checking the appropriate column.

Factor	Deciding Positive Influence	Moderate Positive Influence	Insignificant Influence	Moderate Negative Influence
Availability of capital				
Supply of skilled labor				
Costs of skilled labor				
Supply of unskilled labor				
Cost of unskilled labor				
Union activities				
Supply of fuel and electricity				
Cost of fuel and electricity				

(Continued on following page)

Climate

Personal reasons of management

Transportation network

Political climate

Familiarity with economy

Air quality regulation

Business tax structure

Personal tax structure

Access to raw materials

Access to present customers

Access to growing market

Land costs

3. Some states offer special tax incentives—such as investment tax credits—for new and expanding firms. Did the state tax code of your final choice include a special tax incentive?
Yes __ No __ Don't Know __
If such an incentive was available, please consider the effect of this tax incentive on your location decision.
4. If the tax incentive was *not* offered, would you have located your new business in another state?
Yes __ No __
5. Without the tax incentive, would you have reduced the *amount* of your investment?
Yes __ No __
Please return to: Council of State Planning Agencies

COUNCIL OF STATE PLANNING AGENCIES LOCATION SURVEY
CONFIDENTIAL

In answering the questions in this survey, please refer only to the circumstances relevant in choosing the location for your recent expansion

1. Did you seriously consider expanding by locating a new plant in any other state than your actual expansion? Yes __ No __ (If you answered "No", please skip question 2 and go on to question 3, 4, and 5.)

2. In choosing among states, please think about the factors which led you to choose your final choice. Focus on *differences* between the state you actually chose and those you considered. For example, if *all* of the states you considered had an ample supply of skilled labor, then this had a insignificant effect in choosing between states. Please look over the list of factors below, and indicate how they influenced you by checking the appropriate column.

(Continued on following page) **105**

Factor	Deciding Positive Influence	Moderate Positive Influence	Insignificant Influence	Moderate Negative Influence
Availability of capital				
Economies of scale realized with expansion on-site				
Supply of skilled labor				
Costs of skilled labor				
Supply of unskilled labor				
Cost of unskilled labor				
Union activities				
Maintain intact labor force				
Supply of fuel and electricity				
Cost of fuel and electricity				
Climate				
Personal reasons of management				
Product line or production process not easily divided				
Transportation network				
Political climate				
Familiarity with economy				
Air quality regulation				
Ease of expanding on-site				
Business tax structure				
Personal tax structure				
Access to raw materials				
Access to present customers				
Access to growing market				
Land costs				

3. Some states offer special tax incentives—such as investment tax credits—for new and expanding firms. Did the state tax code of your final choice include a special tax incentive? Yes __ No __ Don't Know __

(Continued on following page)

If such an incentive was available, please consider the effect of this tax incentive on your location decision.
4. If the tax incentive was *not* offered, would you have located your new plant in another state? Yes __ No __
5. Without the tax incentive, would you have reduced the *amount* of your investment? Yes __ No __

Please return to: Council of State Planning Agencies

APPENDIX III

DETAILS ON ECONOMETRIC METHODOLOGY AND RESULTS

This appendix serves to provide additional description of the methodology used, the variables, and results for a number of equations. A great deal more information is available from the author—means and standard deviations for each of the variables and correlation coefficient matrices. In addition to the equations presented in this Appendix, a number of additional equations were tested, and results from those experiments are also available.

DESCRIPTION OF THE VARIABLES

SHARNEWK: The share of new gross investment in depreciable manufacturing assets in a single state for a selected industry in 1977, as reported in the preliminary reports of the Census of Manufacturers 1977. Where a state had no reported investment, its share is represented as zero. For investment in states where disclosure was a problem, the state is not included in the estimated equation because it is impossible to estimate the actual investment.

TAXLOAD: For each industry, a hypothetical average corporation with balance sheets and income statements for 1977 was constructed from IRS and FTC financial reports. For each hypothetical firm, an average tax burden for each state was constructed including corporate profits or franchise taxes, property taxes, capital value taxes, and sales taxes, where applicable. The variable is the dollar amount of taxes paid by the hypothetical corporation in that state. See Appendix I for methodological details as applied to 1980 estimates.

TEMP: For each state, the average annual temperature for the state's largest three cities was calculated. This serves in part as a proxy for weather, and has been found significant in other research.

UNIONGRO: For each state the cumulative rate of growth or decline in the share of the private nonagricultural work force in unions over the period 1970 to 1977 was calculated.

UNION77: Share of the work force in 1977 in unions.

PRODWAGE: For each industry in each state, this variable is the dollar amount of value added divided by the dollar amount of wages paid to production workers. In states with no industry, the national average was substituted.

PRODHOUR: For each industry in each state, this variable represents the dollars of value added divided by the hours worked by production workers. PRODHOUR and PRODWAGE do not appear in the same equation. Same procedure for missing values.

WAGERATE: Wages paid divided by hours worked by production workers. For missing values, the average wage paid by other manufacturing sectors in the state is substituted.

TPPI77: Total state and local taxes with an initial impact on individuals per $1,000 of personal income in 1977.

POPCHANG: For each state, the cumulative rate of growth or decline of population over the period 1970 to 1977 was calculated.

DENSITY: Population per square mile in 1977 for each state, used as a proxy for land costs, which are not recorded by state.

PCPI77: For each state, per capita personal income in 1977, used as a measure of local final consumption demand.

INCCHANG: For each state, cumulative rate of growth or decline of total personal income (not per capita) for the period 1970–1977.

ENERGY: For each state, the dollar cost per million BTU of fuel or electricity actually used in the state in 1976.

SHARHOUR: For each industry in each state, the share of national hours of production worked is used as a measure for the share of the industry already in the state.

WELFARE: For each state, the dollars from state and local revenue sources (Federal welfare was excluded) per $1,000 of personal income expended on general welfare programs.

ORDERST: An alternative measure of business tax burden. Basically, this measure is based on the possibility that it is possible to place business tax burdens in the correct order among states, but have relatively little confidence about the exact number (and hence differences between states which are close in ranking). It was assumed that the actual tax burden by a firm varied with a normal distribution around the estimated figure based on hypothetical balance and income statements. The ranking of states was used to draw a number (in effect) from a table of "order statistics." Because the variance of the normal distribution is not known, it is impossible to use the coefficients to define an elasticity, but the procedure does ensure that the other coefficients are not biased.

EXPECTED SIGNS OF THE COEFFICIENTS

Theory and previous empirical research provides some guide to the expected signs for these variables. A positive coefficient indicates that an increase in the value of the variable is associated with an increase in the share of new capital expenditures, while a negative coefficient indicates the converse.

TAXLOAD: Theoretically no prediction because it depends on the services "purchased" with taxes. Anecdotally, the sign should be negative.

TEMP: Increased temperature is usually thought to be an indication of good weather and thus fewer work interruptions. Previous research has found positive coefficients.

UNIONGRO: Available research indicates that unions are generally successful in increasing wages and that increased labor productivity frequently follows. Theoretically, no prediction. Anecdotally, negative.

UNION77: Same discussion as for UNIONGRO.

PRODWAGE: Increased production per dollar of wages should yield a positive coefficient.

PRODHOUR: Positive.

WAGERATE: Theoretically no prediction is possible, since it depends on productivity. Anecdotally, negative.

TPPI77: As with business tax burden, no theoretical prediction is possible, since it depends on the value of services received. Anecdotally, should be negative.

POPCHANG: Increased labor supply and markets for goods should be an inducement. Positive.

DENSITY: If density increases land costs, should serve as a deterrent. Negative.

PCPI77: As an indicator of the magnitude of final demand, should be positive.

INCCHANG: If used as a predictor of future market growth, positive.

ENERGY: As a cost of production, should be negative.

SHARHOUR: With adjustment costs needed for films starting new locations, the coefficient should be positive.

WELFARE: As a redistributive expenditure with no direct benefits for businesses, should have a negative coefficient.

ORDERST: As with business tax burden, theoretically no prediction, but anecdotally should be negative.

PROCEDURES USED The equations for each industry were estimated using the ordinary least squares option within the Statistical Package for the Social Services (SPSS). While a large number of different regressions were run, only a small proportion are shown here (the remainder are available on request from the author). The two business tax burden variables—TAXLOAD and ORDERST—were used as alternates, with the results from running both equations presented here. Because of the very large number of variables tested, and the small number of observations, it was unreasonable to expect statistical significance at normal levels of confidence (usually the .05 level) in very many instances. SPSS has an option which allows the researcher to select some predetermined level of confidence, allowing all variables with a level of significance lower than that determined to be excluded from the final

111

form of the equations. The higher the level of confidence required, the fewer variables that typically remain. The cost of excluding variables, even with a low level of significance, is to bias the coefficients estimated for the remaining variables. This cost becomes more serious if the criterion used is quite strict. In this case, however, the criteron used was only that variables whose level of significance was at least .50 were retained in the equation. This means that, given certain statistical assumptions, there is a probability of at least 50 percent that the actual coefficient for a variable is different than zero.

PRESENTATION OF RESULTS   Empirical results are shown for each of thirteen industries examined. For each industry, there are potentially two sets of results—one each for equations using TAXLOAD or ORDERST. Where both business tax burden measures are excluded from the final equation, there is no difference among results, and only one table is presented for the industry. For each regression, three summary statistics are provided: adjusted R^2, the overall F statistic, and the level of significance of the overall F statistic. For each independent variable included in the final equation, the coefficient, standard error, significance, elasticity, and contribution to R^2 (note: not to adjusted R^2, which is typically somewhat lower) are displayed.

SIC 20: Food and   Neither TAXLOAD nor ORDERST
Kindred Products   exert a significant influence on the investment patterns in the food industry. The existing location of the industry, as represented by SHARHOUR, dominates all other factors. However, with an adjusted R^2 of .570, a substantial portion of interstate variation remains unexplained. The most likely excluded factor of importance is the location of agricultural output.

Table 3-1
Food and Kindred Products
(TAXLOAD and ORDERST Excluded)

Adjusted R^2: .570		Overall F Statistic: 32.16		Significance: .000	
Independent Variable	Coefficient	Standard Error	Significance	Elasticity	R^2 Contribution
SHARHOUR	.881	.111	0	.881	.576
TPP177	-.176E-03	.150E-03	.247	-.647	.013
Constant	.160E-01	.113E-01	.166		

SIC 22: Textile Mill Products
While TAXLOAD is included in the equation with a negative coefficient, its coefficient is not significant. At the .05 level of significance, only SHARHOUR is significant, and dominates the equation in terms of contribution to R^2. At the .10 level of significance, ENERGY is also significant, but with an unexpected positive coefficient. Its contribution to R^2 is quite small.

With ORDERST substituted for TAXLOAD, the results are quite similar. The adjusted R^2 is identical, and the overall F statistic very similar. ENERGY becomes significant at the .05 level, while INCCHANG becomes significant at the .10 level, with a positive coefficient and high elasticity. SHARHOUR continues to account for almost all of the R^2. ORDERST is negative, but insignificant.

Table 3-2
Textile Mill Products
(TAXLOAD Included)

Adjusted R^2: .972		Overall F Statistic: 157.854		Significance: .000	
Independent Variable	Coefficient	Standard Error	Significance	Elasticity	R^2 Contribution
SHARHOUR	.987	.322E-01	0	.985	.971
TEMP	.190E-03	.195E-03	.336	.471	.001
ENERGY	.567E-02	.297E-02	.065	.584	.001
INCCHANGE	.341E-01	.206E-01	.106	1.332	.001
UNIONGRO	-.101E-01	.135E-01	.459	.053	.001
WAGERATE	-.164E-02	.142E-02	.255	-.336	.001
PCP177	.316E-05	.215E-05	.150	.974	.001
UNION77	-.333E-03	.227E-03	.152	-.322	.000
TAXLOAD	-.858E-08	.658E-08	.201	-.054	.001
POPCHANG	-.261E-03	.211E-03	.225	-.107	.001
Constant	-.561E-01	.294E-01	.064		

SIC 26: Paper and Allied Products
SHARHOUR and WAGERATE are the the only significant variables. SHARHOUR accounts for over 40 percent of the interstate variation while WAGERATE accounts for nearly 20 percent. Both coefficients are positive. The adjusted R^2 is .684, and would probably be increased if a variable reflecting forest acreage were included. TAXLOAD is excluded from the truncated equation.

ORDERST, in contrast, is included in the final equation when substituted for TAXLOAD. Otherwise, the results are very similar, with only SHARHOUR and WAGERATE significant and dominating the determination of R^2.

Table 3-3
Textile Mill Products
(ORDERST Included)

Adjusted R^2: .972 *Overall F Statistic: 141.748* *Significance: .000*

Independent Variable	Coefficient	Standard Error	Significance	Elasticity	R^2 Contribution
SHARHOUR	.977	.341E-01	0	.974	.971
TEMP	.101E-03	.239E-03	.674	.251	.001
ENERGY	.626E-02	.303E-02	.047	.645	.001
INCCHANGE	.429E-01	.230E-01	.071	1.676	.001
UNIONGRO	-.143E-01	.136E-01	.299	-.075	.001
WAGERATE	-.212E-02	.145E-02	.155	-.433	.001
PCP177	.284E-05	.212E-05	.189	.875	.001
UNION77	-.332E-03	.226E-03	.150	-.321	.000
ORDERST	-.240E-02	.178E-02	.187	-.002	.001
POPCHANG	-.253E-03	.215E-03	.247	-.104	.001
TPP177	.919E-04	.112E-03	.418	.321	.000
Constant	-.644E-01	.366E-01	.087		

Table 3-4
Paper and Allied Products
(TAXLOAD Excluded)

Adjusted R^2: .684 *Overall F Statistic: 13.198* *Significance: .000*

Independent Variable	Coefficient	Standard Error	Significance	Elasticity	R^2 Contribution
SHARHOUR	.868	.145	0	.862	.432
WAGERATE	.878E-02	.188E-02	.000	2.149	.197
WELFARE	-.109E-01	.781E-02	.172	-.453	.065
PCP177	-.272E-05	.306E-05	.379	-.839	.015
TEMP	.265E-03	.370E-03	.479	.649	.009
UNIONGRO	.260E-01	.208E-01	.220	.130	.005
ENERGY	-.470E-02	.403E-02	.251	-.494	.077
PRODWAGE	-.164E-03	.198E-03	.413	-.062	.005
Constant	-.207E-01	.292E-01	.483	-.062	.005

SIC 28: Chemicals and Allied Products The variables included in the equations for the chemical industry account for just over half of the variation in investment shares among states. TAXLOAD is excluded from the truncated equation. As with the paper industry, SHARHOUR and WAGERATE enter with a significant, and positive coefficient. UNION77 is almost significant at the .10 level with a negative coefficient, and accounts for over 9 percent of the R^2.

Table 3-5
Paper and Allied Products
(ORDERST Included)

Adjusted R^2: .689   Overall F Statistic: 13.488   Significance: .000

Independent Variable	Coefficient	Standard Error	Significance	Elasticity	R^2 Contribution
SHARHOUR	.859	.142	0	.854	.438
WAGERATE	.862E-02	.187E-02	.000	2.374	.197
WELFARE	-.109E-01	.715E-02	.135	-.454	.065
PCP177	-.240E-05	.304E-05	.436	-.739	.015
ORDERST	-.254E-02	.240E-02	.296	-.004	.011
PRODWAGE	-.215E-03	.186E-03	.255	-.081	.005
UNIONGRO	.246E-01	.206E-01	.241	.123	.005
ENERGY	-.466E-02	.400E-02	.251	-.490	.009
Constant	-.731E-02	.208E-01	.728		

With ORDERST substituted for TAXLOAD, the business tax measure does enter the final equation, and is significant at the .10 level. While its coefficient is negative, the elasticity of investment share with respect to ORDERST is quite small, at -.020, indicating that an increase in the value of ORDERST of 1 percent would reduce a state's share of investment by .02 percent of the average investment share. UNION77 becomes significant at the .05 level, with a quite high negative elasticity. This does not indicate a search for low wages, as WAGERATE remains significant and has a quite high positive elasticity. ENERGY becomes significant at the .05 level, and has a negative coefficient. However, variation in energy prices only accounts for about 3 percent of variation in investment shares.

Table 3-6
Chemicals and Allied Products
(TAXLOAD Excluded)

Adjusted R^2: .515   Overall F Statistic: 7.819   Significance: .000

Independent Variable	Coefficient	Standard Error	Significance	Elasticity	R^2 Contribution
SHARHOUR	.960	.253	.001	.958	.288
WAGERATE	.243E-01	.861E-02	.003	7.203	.132
UNION77	-.141E-02	.853E-03	.106	-1.359	.094
UNIONGRO	.869E-01	.546E-01	.120	.443	.021
ENERGY	-.163E-01	.976E-02	.104	-.173	.035
PRODWAGE	.485E-03	.371E-03	.198	.266	.011
TEMP	.866E-03	.904E-03	.344	2.146	.010
Constant	-.132	.817E-01	.115		

Table 3-7
Chemicals and Allied Products
(ORDERST Included)

Adjusted R^2: .536   Overall F Statistic: 7.505   Significance: .000

Independent Variable	Coefficient	Standard Error	Significance	Elasticity	R^2 Contribution
SHARHOUR	.940	.246	.000	.937	.288
WAGERATE	.227E-01	.758E-02	.005	6.724	.132
UNION77	-.163E-02	.715E-03	.028	-1.570	.094
ORDERST	-.982E-02	.572E-02	.094	-.020	.024
PRODWAGE	.570E-03	.357E-03	.119	.312	.018
UNIONGRO	.839E-01	.517E-01	.113	.428	.016
ENERGY	-.262E-01	.125E-01	.042	-2.758	.030
DENSITY	.435E-04	.379E-04	.259	.306	.014
Constant	-.544E-01	.588E-01	.361		

SIC 29: Petroleum and Coal Products The equations for the petroleum industry explain less than half of the variation in investment shares. This may reflect access to port facilities and air quality laws, which are difficult to capture in variables. SHARHOUR and WAGERATE dominate the results, each with positive coefficients. WAGERATE contributes slightly more than SHARHOUR to R^2, and has a substantially higher elasticity. TAXLOAD is excluded from the final equation. PRODWAGE is positive and significant at the .10 level, but contributes less than 3 percent to R^2.

The results change somewhat when ORDERST is substituted for TAXLOAD. ORDERST enters the equation with a negative coefficient significant at the .10 level. The response of investment share, however, is quite inelastic. Variations in business tax burden account for about 4 percent of variation in investment share. PRODWAGE ceases to be significant, while UNION77, with a negative coefficient, becomes significant at the .10 level.

SIC 30: Rubber and Miscellaneous Plastic Products The equations explain over 95 percent of the variation among states in investment shares. SHARHOUR, TAXLOAD, ENERGY, INCCHANG, POPCHANG, and DENSITY are each significant at the .05 level, while UNIONGRO is significant at the .10 level. SHARHOUR dominates the results accounting for over 90 percent of the R^2. TAXLOAD, as expected from anecdotal evidence, has a negative coefficient, but accounts for less than 1 percent of R^2. ENERGY, somewhat surprisingly, has a positive coefficient. INCCHANG has a positive coefficient, but

Table 3-8
Petroleum and Coal Products
(TAXLOAD Excluded)

Adjusted R^2: .431   Overall F Statistic: 5.860   Significance: .000

Independent Variable	Coefficient	Standard Error	Significance	Elasticity	R^2 Contribution
SHARHOUR	1.599	.355	.000	1.584	.199
WAGERATE	.300E-01	.661E-02	.000	9.308	.227
PRODWAGE	.184E-02	.106E-02	.089	.789	.027
TEMP	.875E-03	.148E-02	.559	2.167	.023
UNIONGRO	.190	.114	.104	-1.025	.012
UNION77	-.198E-02	.152E-02	.202	-1.895	.024
TPPI77	-.504E-03	.678E-03	.461	-1.775	.007
Constant	-.177	.125	.165		

Table 3-9
Petroleum and Coal Products
(ORDERST Included)

Adjusted R^2: .459   Overall F Statistic: 6.462   Significance: .000

Independent Variable	Coefficient	Standard Error	Significance	Elasticity	R^2 Contribution
SHARHOUR	1.500	.347	.000	1.486	.199
WAGERATE	.319E-01	.642E-02	.000	9.883	.227
ORDERST	-.180E-01	.958E-02	.067	-.013	.042
PRODWAGE	.155E-02	.102E-02	.137	.663	.021
UNIONGRO	.144	.117	.223	.778	.011
UNION77	-.267E-02	.146E-02	.075	-2.563	.034
DENSITY	.432E-04	.488E-04	.382	.300	.009
Constant	-.173	.469E-01	.001		

accounts for less than 1 percent of R^2. POPCHANG and DENSITY each have negative coefficients, and contribute trivially to R^2. It is conceivable that POPCHANG has a negative coefficient due to the possible effects of pollution from the industry on the residential choices of residents.

When ORDERST is substituted for TAXLOAD, the results are quite similar. Adjusted R^2 remains the same, and no variables change from significant to insignificant, or vice versa.

SIC 32: Stone, Clay, and Glass Products   Both TAXLOAD and ORDERST are excluded from the equation due to lack of significance. SHARHOUR dominates the   *117*

Table 3-10
Rubber and Miscellaneous Plastic Products
(TAXLOAD Included)

Adjusted R^2: .958   Overall F Statistic: 118.800   Significance: .000

Independent Variable	Coefficient	Standard Error	Significance	Elasticity	R^2 Contribution
SHARHOUR	.996	.371E-01	0	.993	.931
TAXLOAD	-.650E-07	.237E-07	.009	-.176	.009
UNION77	-.223E-03	.134E-03	.106	-.222	.004
ENERGY	.953E-02	.215E-02	.000	1.016	.004
INCCHANG	.377E-01	.135E-01	.008	1.503	.008
UNIONGRO	-.155E-01	.868E-02	.082	.080	.004
POPCHANG	-.332E-03	.153E-03	.036	-.134	.002
DENSITY	-.129E-04	.593E-05	.036	-.091	.003
PCP177	-.158E-05	.133E-05	.243	.498	.001
Constant	-.525E-01	.187E-01	.008		

Table 3-11
Rubber and Miscellaneous Plastic Products
(ORDERST Included)

Adjusted R^2: .959   Overall F Statistic: 120.922   Significance: .000

Independent Variable	Coefficient	Standard Error	Significance	Elasticity	R^2 Contribution
SHARHOUR	.997	.368E-01	.000	.994	.931
ORDERST	-.263E-02	.913E-03	.007	-.004	.011
ENERGY	.934E-02	.214E-02	.000	.996	.004
INCCHANG	.348E-01	.136E-01	.015	1.390	.008
UNIONGRO	-.155E-01	.860E-02	.079	.080	.006
DENSITY	-.124E-04	.589E-05	.042	-.088	.002
POPCHANG	-.308E-03	.149E-03	.047	-.124	.002
PCPI77	.149E-05	.132E-05	.266	.470	.001
UNION77	-.208E-03	.133E-03	.125	-.207	.001
Constant	-.533E-01	.184E-01	.006		

equation, with a positive coefficient, and a contribution to R^2 of over 80 percent. TEMP is the only other significant coefficient, and as expected is positive. However, it accounts for less than 3 percent of interstate variation in investment shares.

SIC 33: Primary Metal Industries   Both TAXLOAD and ORDERST are excluded from the equation due to lack of significance. Only SHARHOUR is significant at the .05 level, and contributes over 80 percent of R^2. This may

Table 3-12
Stone, Clay, and Glass Products
(TAXLOAD and ORDERST Excluded)

Adjusted R^2: .863   Overall F Statistic: 43.150   Significance: .000

Independent Variable	Coefficient	Standard Error	Significance	Elasticity	R^2 Contribution
SHARHOUR	.876	.660E-01	.000	.875	.837
TEMP	.479E-03	.211E-03	.029	1.236	.026
DENSITY	-.121E-04	.743E-05	.112	-.086	.007
PRODWAGE	.215E-02	.335E-02	.525	.353	.003
UNION77	-.306E-03	.210E-03	.152	.309	.003
PCPI77	.272E-05	.218E-05	.220	.874	.003
POPCHANG	-.246E-03	.221E-03	.272	-.106	.004
Constant	-.383E-01	.182E-01	.041		

Table 3-13
Primary Metal Industries
(TAXLOAD and ORDERST Excluded)

Adjusted R^2: .841   Overall F Statistic: 29.523   Significance: .000

Independent Variable	Coefficient	Standard Error	Significance	Elasticity	R^2 Contribution
SHARHOUR	.807	.772	.000	.783	.820
TPPI77	-.244E-03	.158E-03	.133	-.820	.017
WAGERATE	.160E-02	.163E-02	.331	.464	.013
TEMP	.484E-03	.319E-03	.138	1.148	.003
PCPI77	.489E-05	.352E-05	.103	1.709	.003
DENSITY	-.287E-04	.153E-04	.070	-.184	.005
POPCHANG	-.426E-03	.343E-03	.212	-.169	.005
ENERGY	.504E-02	.468E-02	.290	.501	.004
Constant	-.553E-01	.331E-01	.104		

reflect the lack of net new investment in the industry, with most investment occurring at existing locations for maintenance. DENSITY is significant at the .10 level, with a negative coefficient.

SIC 34: Fabricated Metal Products

The equation accounts for almost all of interstate variation in investment shares, with an adjusted R^2 of .978. SHARHOUR accounts for almost all of the variation. WAGERATE has a positive influence, and is significant at the .10 level, while UNION77 has a negative influence, significant at the .10 level. Surprisingly, PRODWAGE has a negative influence, significant at the .10 level.

WAGERATE, UNION77, and PRODWAGE each account for only about 1 percent of R^2. While TAXLOAD is included in the final equation, its coefficient is insignificant.

With ORDERST substituted for TAXLOAD, the overall F statistic increases substantially, although there is little change in R^2. SHARHOUR continues to dominate the equation, accounting for almost all of the interstate variation. ORDERST has a negative coefficient, and is significant at the .05 level. However, the associated elasticity is extremely low. UNION77 and PRODWAGE retain their negative coefficients, but become significant at the .05 level.

Table 3-14
Fabricated Metal Products
(TAXLOAD Included)

Adjusted R^2: .978   Overall F Statistic: 225.337   Significance: .000

Independent Variable	Coefficient	Standard Error	Significance	Elasticity	R^2 Contribution
SHARHOUR	1.016	.323E-01	.000	1.016	.975
ENERGY	-.134E-02	.122E-02	.278	-.143	.003
WAGERATE	.318E-02	.181E-02	.086	.844	.001
UNION77	-.212E-03	.107E-03	.055	-.209	.001
PRODWAGE	-.951E-04	.507E-04	.069	-.027	.001
TPPI77	-.622E-04	.558E-04	.272	-.224	.000
TEMP	-.206E-03	.134E-03	.134	-.520	.001
TAXLOAD	-.264E-07	.293E-07	.373	-.053	.000
WELFARE	.398E-03	.535E-03	.462	.020	.000
Constant	.628E-02	.154E-01	.681		

Table 3-15
Fabricated Metal Products
(ORDERST Included)

Adjusted R^2: .980   Overall F Statistic: 321.130   Significance: .000

Independent Variable	Coefficient	Standard Error	Significance	Elasticity	R^2 Contribution
SHARHOUR	1.025	.310	.000	1.024	.975
ENERGY	-.159E-02	.109E-02	.154	-.169	.003
WAGERATE	.287E-02	.170E-02	.099	.763	.001
UNION77	-.223E-03	.101E-03	.030	-.225	.001
PRODWAGE	-.104E-03	.486E-04	.039	-.030	.001
ORDERST	-.189E-02	.866E-03	.035	-.002	.001
TEMP	-.261E-03	.120E-03	.051	-.661	.002
Constant	.640E-02	.139E-01	.648		

SIC 35: Machinery, Except Electrical Only SHARHOUR is significant, and accounts for over 90 percent of variation in investment shares. This is the only industry, in which TAXLOAD is included in a final equation, while ORDERST is excluded. However, TAXLOAD, with a positive coefficient, is statistically insignificant.

SIC 36: Electric and Electronic Equipment With TAXLOAD included, 95 percent of the variation in investment shares is explained. However, TAXLOAD is insignificant. SHARHOUR dominates the equation, accounting for about 90 percent of R^2. As frequently discussed in the industry, WAGERATE and DENSITY exert negative influences on investment, with WAGERATE exerting a larger relative negative influence. Somewhat surpris-

Table 3-16
Machinery, Except Electrical
(TAXLOAD Included)

Adjusted R^2: .912		Overall F Statistic: 70.589		Significance: .000	
Independent Variable	Coefficient	Standard Error	Significance	Elasticity	R^2 Contribution
SHARHOUR	1.064	.613E-01	0	1.063	.905
POPCHANG	.277E-03	.204E-03	.183	.120	.010
TEMP	.294E-03	.186E-03	.122	.759	.004
PCPI77	.263E-05	.202E-05	.200	.844	.001
UNION77	-.181E-03	.202E-03	.374	-.183	.001
TAXLOAD	.106E-07	.100E-07	.297	.061	.001
INCCHANGE	.131E-01	.160E-01	.401	.532	.001
Constant	-.458E-01	.244E-01	.068		

Table 3-17
Machinery, Except Electrical
(ORDERST Excluded)

Adjusted R^2: .913		Overall F Statistic: 100.148		Significance: .000	
Independent Variable	Coefficient	Standard Error	Significance	Elasticity	R^2 Contribution
SHARHOUR	1.075	.603E-01	.000	1.074	.905
POPCHANG	.272E-03	.199E-03	.179	.118	.010
TEMP	.262E-03	.178E-03	.149	.676	.004
PCPI77	.210E-05	.189E-05	.273	.674	.001
UNION77	-.178E-03	.200E-03	.378	-.180	.001
Constant	-.284E-01	.162E-01	.088		

ingly, WELFARE exerts a positive influence, although it contributes little to R^2. PCPI77, perhaps as a measure of the availability of skilled labor rather than market demand, exerts a positive influence, although it accounts for less than 1 percent of R^2. The results are almost identical when ORDERST is substituted for TAXLOAD.

SIC 37: Transportation Equipment   SHARHOUR, UNION77, WELFARE, WAGERATE, INCCHANG, and PCPI77 are all significant at the .05 level, while

Table 3-18
Electric and Electronic Equipment
(TAXLOAD Included)

Adjusted R^2: .950		*Overall F Statistic: 95.500*		*Significance: .000*	
Independent Variable	*Coefficient*	*Standard Error*	*Significance*	*Elasticity*	*R^2 Contribution*
SHARHOUR	1.118	.567E-01	0	1.114	.906
WAGERATE	-.758E-03	.154E-03	.000	-.219	.030
DENSITY	-.182E-04	.619E-05	.006	-.124	.005
PCPI77	.353E-05	.164E-05	.038	1.086	.003
TEMP	.313E-03	.198E-03	.123	.777	.005
WELFARE	.906E-02	.350E-02	.014	.372	.007
UNION77	-.275E-03	.173E-03	.121	-.267	.001
UNIONGRO	.106E-01	.111E-01	.345	-.056	.001
TAXLOAD	-.103E-07	.145E-07	.483	-.067	.001
Constant	-.351E-01	.178E-01	.057		

Table 3-19
Electric and Electronic Equipment
(ORDERST Included)

Adjusted R^2: .950		*Overall F Statistic: 95.752*		*Significance: .000*	
Independent Variable	*Coefficient*	*Standard Error*	*Significance*	*Elasticity*	*R^2 Contribution*
SHARHOUR	1.121	.571E-01	.000	1.117	.906
WAGERATE	-.753E-03	.155E-03	.000	-.217	.030
DENSITY	-.181E-04	.620E-05	.006	-.123	.005
PCPI77	.348E-05	.165E-05	.041	1.071	.003
TEMP	.290E-03	.213E-03	.181	.720	.005
WELFARE	.906E-02	.349E-02	.014	.371	.007
UNION77	-.285E-03	.177E-03	.116	-.277	.001
UNIONGRO	.111E-01	.110E-01	.321	-.059	.001
ORDERST	-.112E-02	.150E-02	.459	-.001	.001
Constant	-.349E-01	.177E-01	.057		

TAXLOAD and TPPI77 are significant at the .10 level. SHARHOUR, with a positive coefficient, dominates the equation, accounting for over 90 percent of R^2. Only WELFARE, with a negative coefficient, accounts for more than 1 percent of R^2 among the remaining significant variables. TAXLOAD, for the first time, is significant and *positive* although it accounts for only .2 percent of interstate variation. In contrast, personal taxation, as represented by TPPI77, has a negative coefficient, while also contributing very little to R^2.

The results are quite similar when ORDERST is substituted for TAXLOAD. No variables change sign or alter in significance with the substitution. ORDERST, while still positive, remains a very minor contributor to R^2.

Table 3-20
Transportation Equipment
(TAXLOAD Included)

Adjusted R^2: .964		Overall F Statistic: 98.853		Significance: .000	
Independent Variable	Coefficient	Standard Error	Significance	Elasticity	R^2 Contribution
SHARHOUR	1.034	.443E-01	0	1.009	.930
UNION77	.101E-02	.285E-03	.001	.855	.009
WELFARE	-.134E-01	.642E-02	.046	-.481	.015
POPCHANG	-.336E-03	.394E-03	.401	-.094	.007
WAGERATE	.418E-02	.139E-02	.005	1.041	.003
INCCHANG	-.470E-01	.215E-01	.038	-1.512	.001
PCPI77	-.682E-05	.285E-05	.024	-1.765	.002
TAXLOAD	.102E-07	.573E-08	.087	.176	.002
TPPI77	-.310E-03	.175E-03	.088	-.895	.002
PRODWAGE	.699E-04	.493E-04	.167	.843	.002
Constant	.690E-01	.313E-01	.036		

SIC 38: Instruments and Related Products The equation, with TAXLOAD included, accounts for nearly 90 percent of interstate variation. SHARHOUR accounts for nearly all of this, with an elasticity greater than one. Among the remaining variables, only WAGERATE is significant and has a positive coefficient. WAGERATE contributes less than 2 percent to R^2. TAXLOAD, while included in the truncated equation, is insignificant. PCPI77, with a surprising negative coefficient, is significant at the .10 level, but contributes little to R^2.

When ORDERST is substituted for TAXLOAD, the results are very similar. ORDERST has a negative coefficient but is insignificant, while SHARHOUR continues to dominate the equation. *123*

Table 3-21
Transportation Equipment
(ORDERST Included)

Adjusted R^2: .964   Overall F Statistic: 101.081   Significance: .000

Independent Variable	Coefficient	Standard Error	Significance	Elasticity	R^2 Contribution
SHARHOUR	1.024	.437E-01	0	1.00	.930
UNION77	.948E-03	.277E-03	.001	.834	.009
WELFARE	-.134E-01	.635E-02	.045	-.480	.015
POPCHANG	-.314E-03	.389E-03	.426	-.088	.007
WAGERATE	.450E-02	.141E-02	.004	1.119	.003
ORDERST	.369E-02	.189E-02	.061	-.001	.001
PCPI77	-.705E-05	.248E-05	.019	-1.823	.001
INCCHANG	-.461E-01	.212E-01	.038	-1.483	.002
TPPI77	-.326E-03	.174E-03	.073	-.939	.002
PRODWAGE	.787E-04	.490E-04	.120	.048	.002
Constant	.741E-01	.313E-01	.026		

Table 3-22
Instruments and Related Products
(TAXLOAD Included)

Adjusted R^2: .898   Overall F Statistic: 43.008   Significance: .000

Independent Variable	Coefficient	Standard Error	Significance	Elasticity	R^2 Contribution
SHARHOUR	1.387	.946E-01	0	1.350	.876
WAGERATE	.899E-02	.318E-02	.008	1.943	.016
UNION77	-.471E-03	.409E-03	.257	-.414	.010
TAXLOAD	-.708E-07	.507E-07	.172	-.284	.008
TPPI77	.167E-03	.194E-03	.395	.556	.002
PCPI77	-.513E-05	.300E-05	.096	-1.465	.003
PRODWAGE	-.310E-03	.276E-03	.269	-.106	.001
UNIONGRO	.198E-01	.201E-01	.332	-.006	.002
POPCHANG	.308E-03	.360E-03	.399	.118	.002
Constant	-.134E-01	.206E-01	.518		

SUMMARY OF ECONOMETRIC RESULTS

As previously discussed, the strength of these results is limited by reliance on a single year's cross sectional data. However, even with this constraint, the results appear quite striking.

For the most part, the single most important determinant of current investment in an industry is the current location of employment. Only

Table 3-23
Instruments and Related Products
(ORDERST Included)

Adjusted R^2: .897   Overall F Statistic: 42.818   Significance: .000

Independent Variable	Coefficient	Standard Error	Significance	Elasticity	R^2 Contribution
SHARHOUR	1.390	.947E-01	0	1.352	.876
WAGERATE	.902E-02	.319E-02	.008	1.948	.016
UNION77	-.462E-03	.409E-03	.267	-.407	.010
ORDERST	-.393E-02	.293E-02	.188	-.001	.007
TPP177	.163E-03	.194E-03	.407	.543	.002
PCP177	-.520E-05	.300E-05	.092	-1.486	.004
PRODWAGE	-.312E-03	.267E-03	.267	-.107	.001
UNIONGRO	.198E-01	.202E-01	.335	-.106	.002
POPCHANG	.292E-03	.365E-03	.430	.112	.002
Constant	-.193E-01	.216E-01	.379		

a portion of this can be interpreted as resulting from expansion or rehabilitation of existing plant. This result holds regardless of the measure used for business tax burden. For the most part, the elasticity of investment share with respect to employment share is in the close neighborhood of one, meaning that a 1 percent increase in employment share is generally accompanied by a 1 percent increase in investment share.

APPENDIX IV

PROCEDURES USED IN THE BENEFIT-COST ANALYSIS OF TAX INCENTIVES

This Appendix describes in more detail the methods used to develop the benefit-cost estimates of Chapter Four. The goal of those estimates was to determine whether or not tax incentives were reasonable public investments. This appendix does not duplicate the general discussion of public investment principles which appears in Chapter Two, nor does it present all of the calculations involved in estimating the rate of of return on tax revenues foregone. Instead it focuses on showing how certain critical figures were derived. In particular, it explains:

1. the estimate of new income generated by manufacturing investment;
2. the estimate of new investment generated by a cut in overall business tax burden; and
3. the tax loss associated with a reduction in overall tax burden.

ESTIMATING NEW INCOME GENERATED BY MANUFACTURING INVESTMENT In the public investment analysis, benefits are defined as the new income arising out of the manufacturing investment which accrues to state citizens. Since the various investment tax credits are usually based on depreciable investment, it is useful to relate income to depreciable investment. Income has three components: payroll, pretax profits, and interest. The payroll figure was obtained by calculating the ratio of payroll to value of shipments (a close proxy for sales) for all manufacturing industries from the 1977 Preliminary Census of Manufacturers. This ratio was then applied to the sales total from the aggregate income statement for manufacturing firms available by summing the quarterly figures reported in the *Quarterly Financial Reports* of the Federal Trade Commission. This resulted in an estimate of payroll for the aggregate income statement, which could be directly compared to net depreciable assets for the parallel aggregate balance sheet. The ratio of pretax profits to net depreciable assets was more straightforward, relying solely upon those aggregates from the 1977 FTC reports. The ratio of interest payments to net depreciable assets was obtained by assuming that the average interest rate on all liabilities in 1977 was 7 percent. This interest rate resulted in an estimate of total interest payments, which could then be compared to net depreciable assets. When rounded to two decimal places, this procedure resulted in the following estimates of income for each dollar of net depreciable investment: $.97 of payroll, $.36 of pre-tax profits, and $.11 of interest or a total of $1.44 of annual income per dollar of initial depreciable investment. This ratio will naturally vary among industries, states, and individual projects.

ESTIMATING THE NEW INVESTMENT GENERATED BY A GENERAL BUSINESS TAX CUT
The econometric results were used to analyze the effects on specific sectors of a lasting reduction in the overall tax burden, as opposed to a specific investment tax credit. The analysis was carried out for both the TAXLOAD and ORDERST tax burden variables. The critical figure in the analysis was the estimate of elasticity generated by the regression analysis. The elasticity of investment share in the Rubber industry was estimated to be –.176, meaning that for the mean state, a reduction of 1 percent of tax burden would result in an increase in investment share of .176 percent (note: not .176 percentage points). Thus, a state lowering its business taxes on future income and assets in the Rubber industry should expect its share of national investment to increase to 1.00176 times its current share. For the Rubber industry in 1977, with national investment of $1573.7 million, this represents only $58,930 in new investment for the mean state. To this amount of new investment, the previously determined ratio of new income to investment can be applied to estimate benefits. The same methodology is used when elasticities based on ORDERST are used.

ESTIMATING THE TAX LOSS ASSOCIATED WITH A REDUCTION IN TAX BURDEN
Since it was assumed that the tax reduction would go to income and assets from new investment only, the tax loss should be calculated by estimating some ratio of total state and local tax payments to depreciable investment. For the average manufacturing firm in 1977, 9.04 percent of depreciable investment went to state and local taxes, based on comparing the net depreciable assets in an average manufacturing firm with the average tax burden for the average manufacturing firm. The cost of the new investment must be the tax loss due to the lower tax rates on income and assets from all new investments, not just the induced investment. For the *127*

mean state, a reduction of 1 percent in taxes resulting from the new investment would be only $30,135.